Book One

Action Lab Entertainment

Molly Danger, Book One
Published by Action Lab Entertainment, inc.

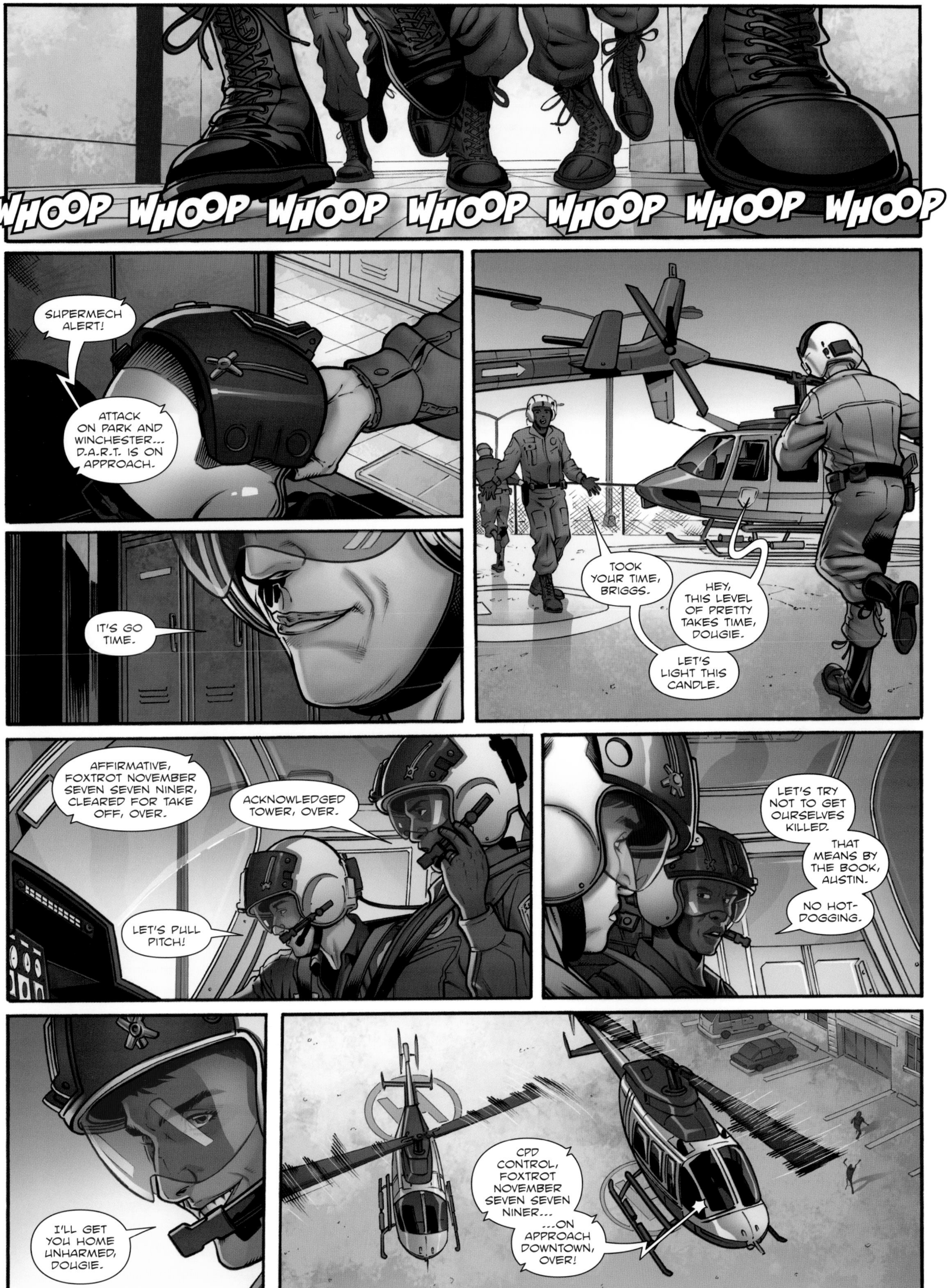
WHOOP WHOOP WHOOP WHOOP WHOOP WHOOP WHOOP
SUPERMECH ALERT!
ATTACK ON PARK AND WINCHESTER... D.A.R.T. IS ON APPROACH.
TOOK YOUR TIME, BRIGGS.
HEY, THIS LEVEL OF PRETTY TAKES TIME, DOUGIE.
LET'S LIGHT THIS CANDLE.
IT'S GO TIME.
AFFIRMATIVE, FOXTROT NOVEMBER SEVEN SEVEN NINER, CLEARED FOR TAKE OFF, OVER.
ACKNOWLEDGED TOWER, OVER.
LET'S PULL PITCH!
LET'S TRY NOT TO GET OURSELVES KILLED.
THAT MEANS BY THE BOOK, AUSTIN.
NO HOT-DOGGING.
I'LL GET YOU HOME UNHARMED, DOUGIE.
CPD CONTROL, FOXTROT NOVEMBER SEVEN SEVEN NINER... ...ON APPROACH DOWNTOWN, OVER!

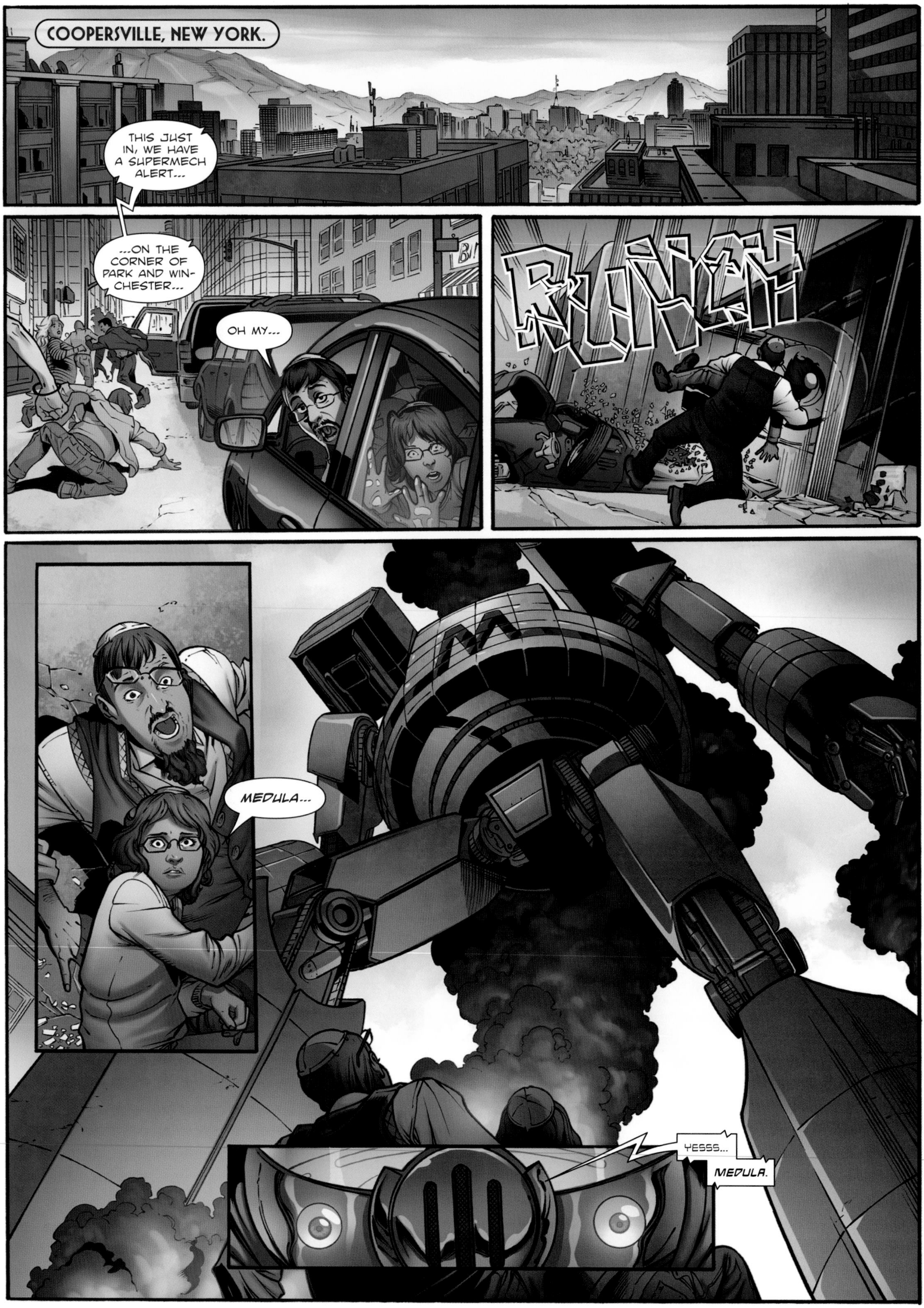
COOPERSVILLE, NEW YORK.
THIS JUST IN, WE HAVE A SUPERMECH ALERT...
...ON THE CORNER OF PARK AND WIN-CHESTER...
OH MY...
MEDULA...
YESSS...
MEDULA.

CITIZENS OF COOPERSVILLE, YOUR *LIBERATION* IS AT HAND!

I WILL FREE YOU FROM THE *BANALITY* OF YOUR LIVES.

I WILL *SAVE YOU* FROM THE PRISON OF FLESH.

FOOOM

FOOOM

FOOOM

FOOOOM

FOOM

KROOM

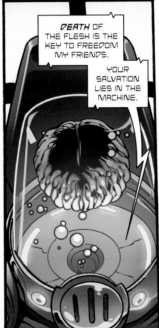

DEATH OF THE FLESH IS THE KEY TO FREEDOM MY FRIENDS.

YOUR SALVATION LIES IN THE MACHINE.

FOOOM

FOOOM

FOOOOM

KABOOM

D.A.R.T. COMMAND TO MOLLYMOBILE 1, WHAT'S YOUR 20?

PACKAGE EN ROUTE TO DZ.

COPY THAT, MOLLYMOBILE 1.

HE'S *RANTING* AGAIN.

LET'S SHUT THIS DOWN WITH A LITTLE *FINESSE*, PACKAGE.

I'M THE PRINCESS OF FINESSE, COMMAND.

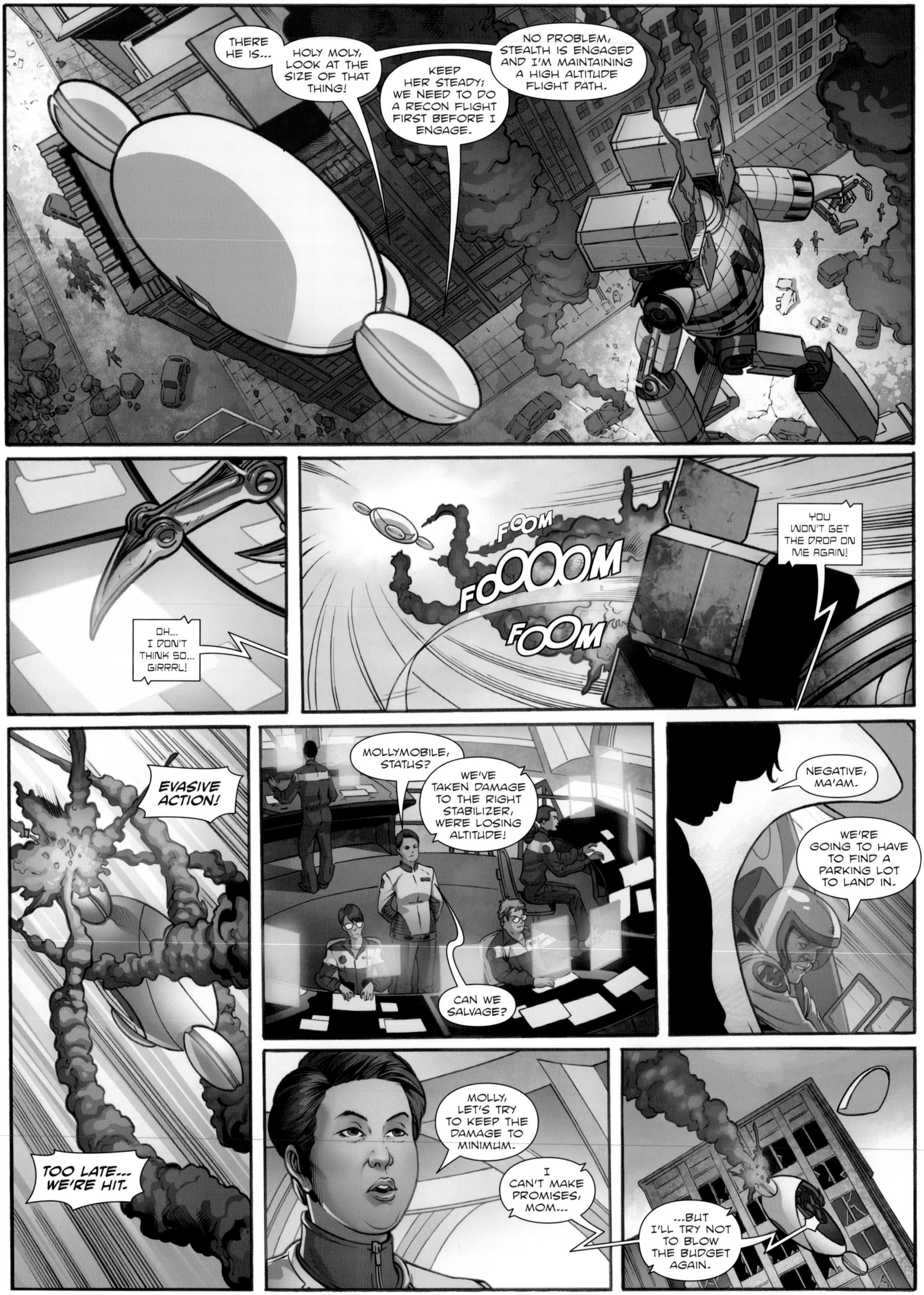

THERE HE IS...
HOLY MOLY, LOOK AT THE SIZE OF THAT THING!
KEEP HER STEADY; WE NEED TO DO A RECON FLIGHT FIRST BEFORE I ENGAGE.
NO PROBLEM, STEALTH IS ENGAGED AND I'M MAINTAINING A HIGH ALTITUDE FLIGHT PATH.
OH... I DON'T THINK SO... GIRRRL!
FOOM
FOOOOOM
FOOM
YOU WON'T GET THE DROP ON ME AGAIN!
EVASIVE ACTION!
TOO LATE... WE'RE HIT.
MOLLYMOBILE, STATUS?
WE'VE TAKEN DAMAGE TO THE RIGHT STABILIZER, WERE LOSING ALTITUDE!
CAN WE SALVAGE?
NEGATIVE, MA'AM.
WE'RE GOING TO HAVE TO FIND A PARKING LOT TO LAND IN.
MOLLY, LET'S TRY TO KEEP THE DAMAGE TO MINIMUM.
I CAN'T MAKE PROMISES, MOM...
...BUT I'LL TRY NOT TO BLOW THE BUDGET AGAIN.

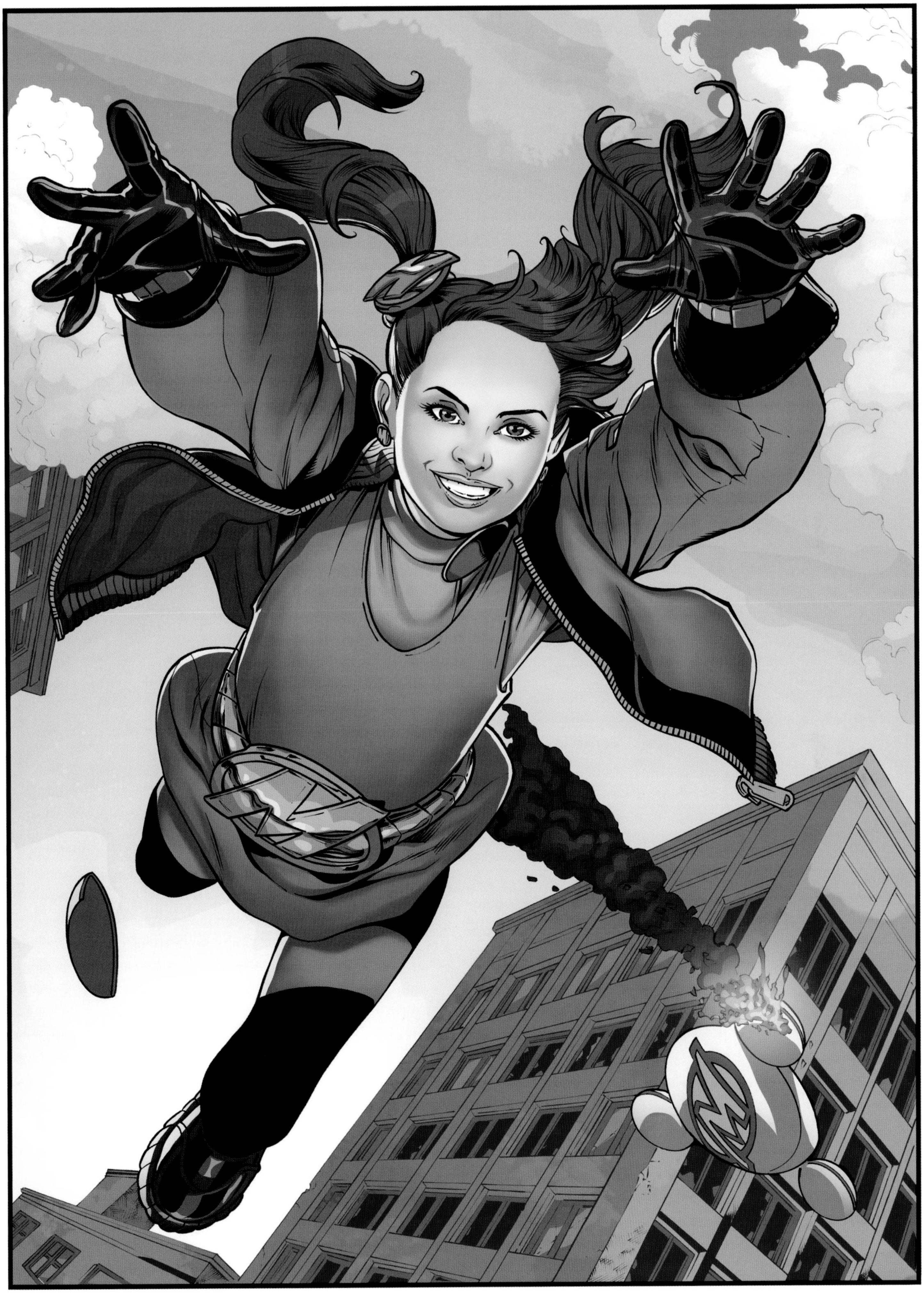

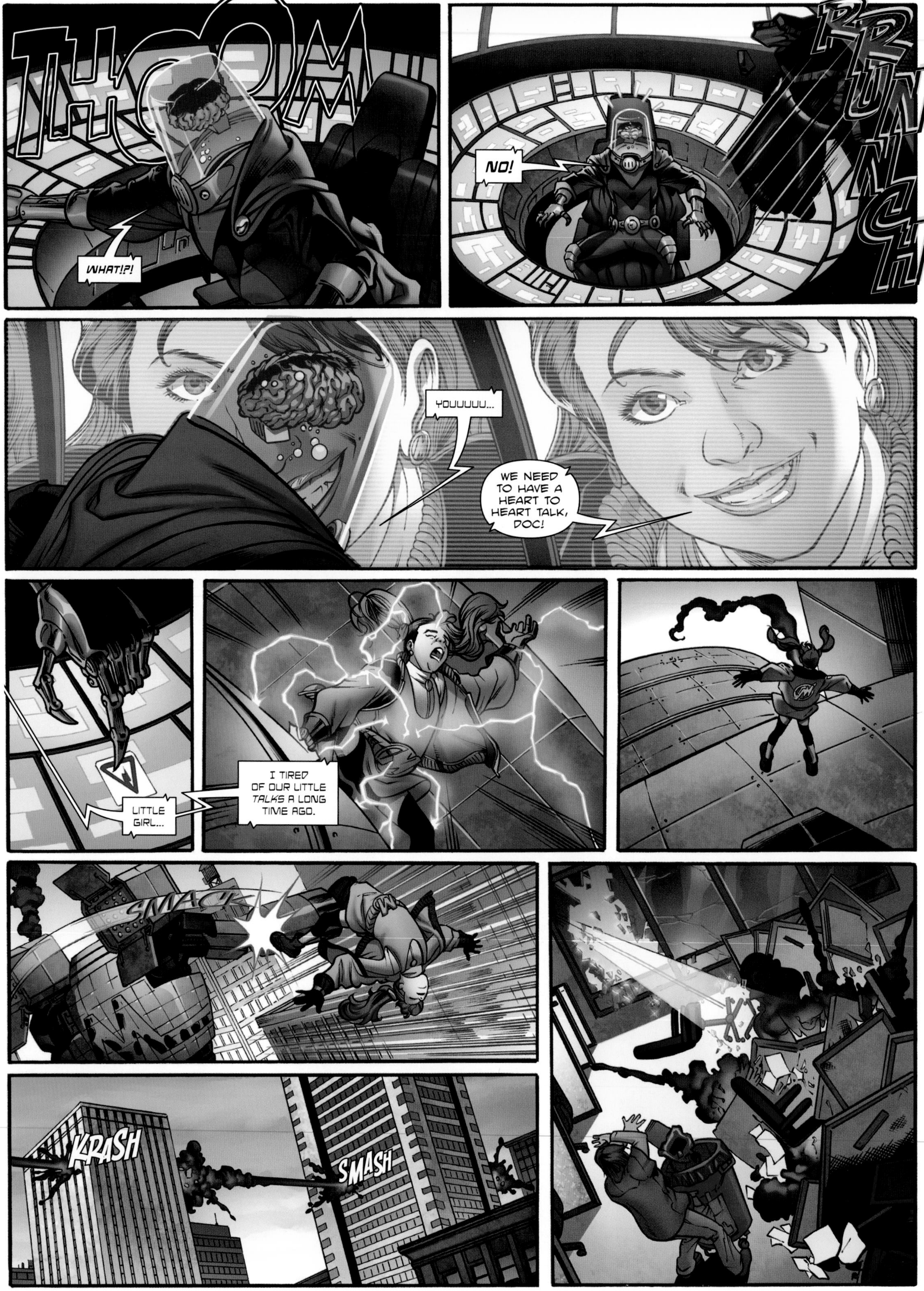
THOOM
WHAT!?!
NO!
PRUNNCH
YOUUUUU...
WE NEED TO HAVE A HEART TO HEART TALK, DOC!
LITTLE GIRL...
I TIRED OF OUR LITTLE *TALKS* A LONG TIME AGO.
SMACK
KRASH
SMASH

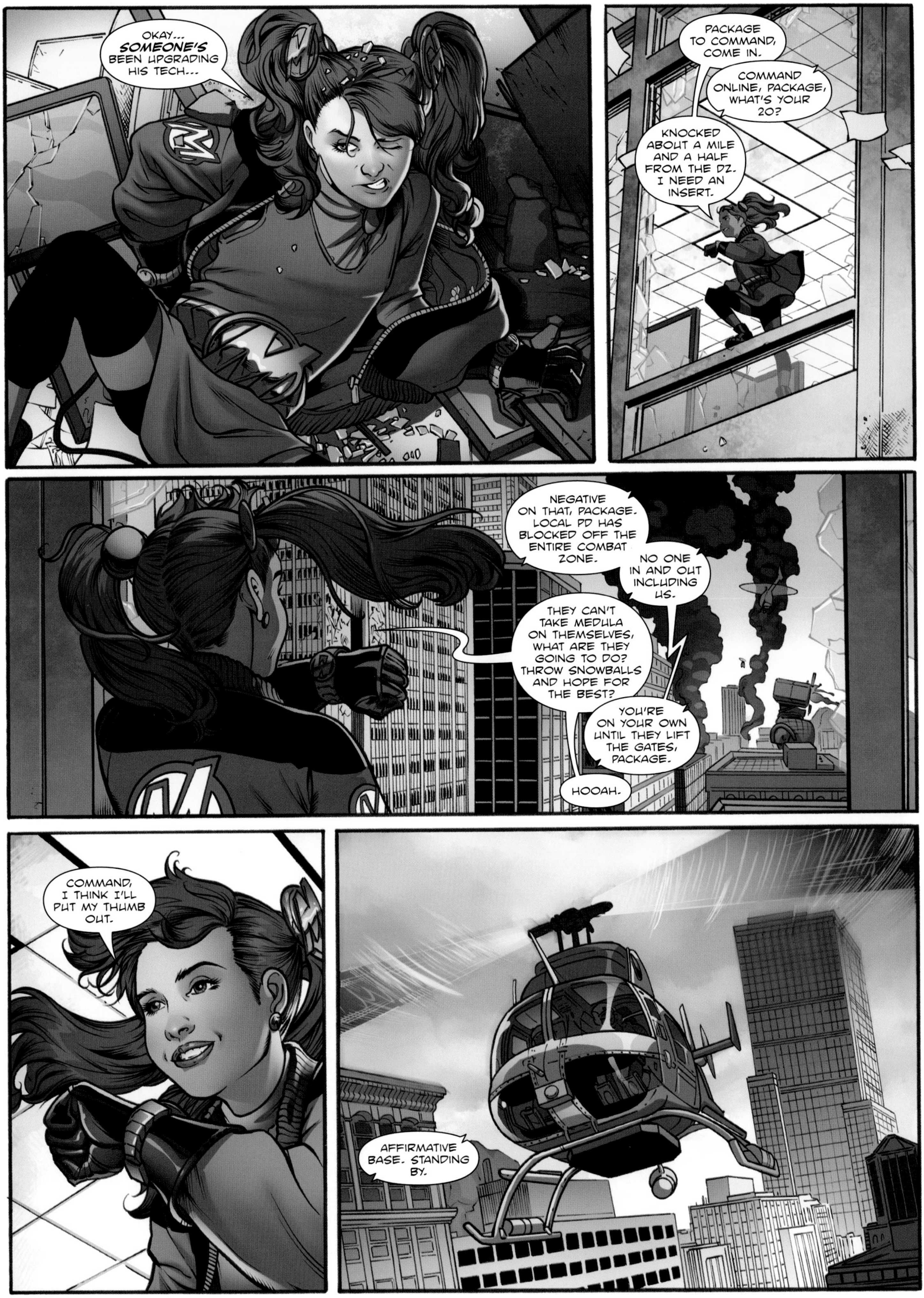
OKAY... SOMEONE'S BEEN UPGRADING HIS TECH...
PACKAGE TO COMMAND, COME IN.
COMMAND ONLINE, PACKAGE, WHAT'S YOUR 20?
KNOCKED ABOUT A MILE AND A HALF FROM THE DZ. I NEED AN INSERT.
NEGATIVE ON THAT, PACKAGE. LOCAL PD HAS BLOCKED OFF THE ENTIRE COMBAT ZONE.
NO ONE IN AND OUT INCLUDING US.
THEY CAN'T TAKE MEDULA ON THEMSELVES, WHAT ARE THEY GOING TO DO? THROW SNOWBALLS AND HOPE FOR THE BEST?
YOU'RE ON YOUR OWN UNTIL THEY LIFT THE GATES, PACKAGE.
HOOAH.
COMMAND, I THINK I'LL PUT MY THUMB OUT.
AFFIRMATIVE BASE. STANDING BY.

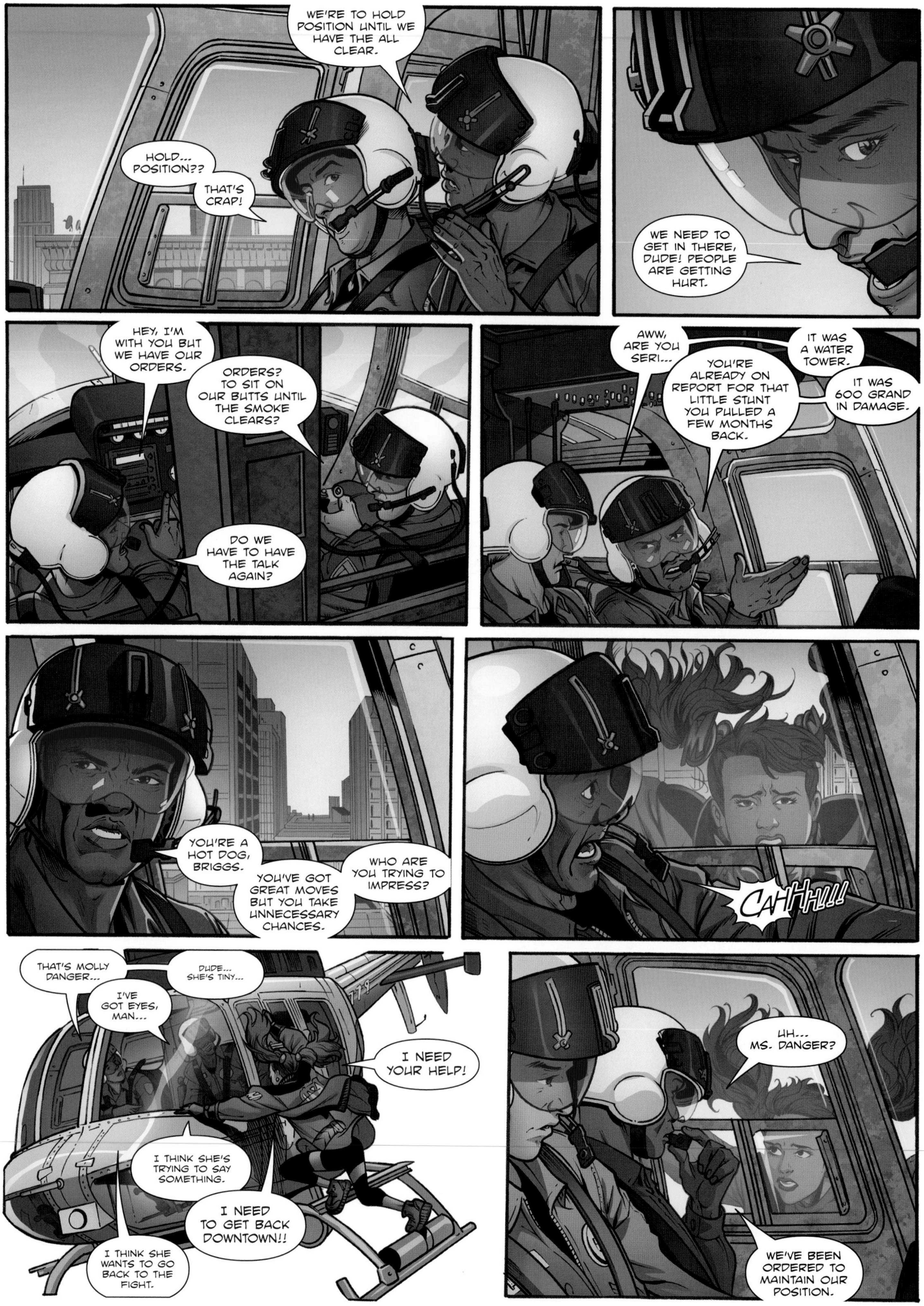
WE'RE TO HOLD POSITION UNTIL WE HAVE THE ALL CLEAR.
HOLD... POSITION??
THAT'S CRAP!
WE NEED TO GET IN THERE, DUDE! PEOPLE ARE GETTING HURT.
HEY, I'M WITH YOU BUT WE HAVE OUR ORDERS.
ORDERS? TO SIT ON OUR BUTTS UNTIL THE SMOKE CLEARS?
DO WE HAVE TO HAVE THE TALK AGAIN?
AWW, ARE YOU SERI...
YOU'RE ALREADY ON REPORT FOR THAT LITTLE STUNT YOU PULLED A FEW MONTHS BACK.
IT WAS A WATER TOWER.
IT WAS 600 GRAND IN DAMAGE.
YOU'RE A HOT DOG, BRIGGS.
YOU'VE GOT GREAT MOVES BUT YOU TAKE UNNECESSARY CHANCES.
WHO ARE YOU TRYING TO IMPRESS?
CAHHH!!!
THAT'S MOLLY DANGER...
DUDE... SHE'S TINY...
I'VE GOT EYES, MAN...
I NEED YOUR HELP!
I THINK SHE'S TRYING TO SAY SOMETHING.
I NEED TO GET BACK DOWNTOWN!!
I THINK SHE WANTS TO GO BACK TO THE FIGHT.
UH... MS. DANGER?
WE'VE BEEN ORDERED TO MAINTAIN OUR POSITION.

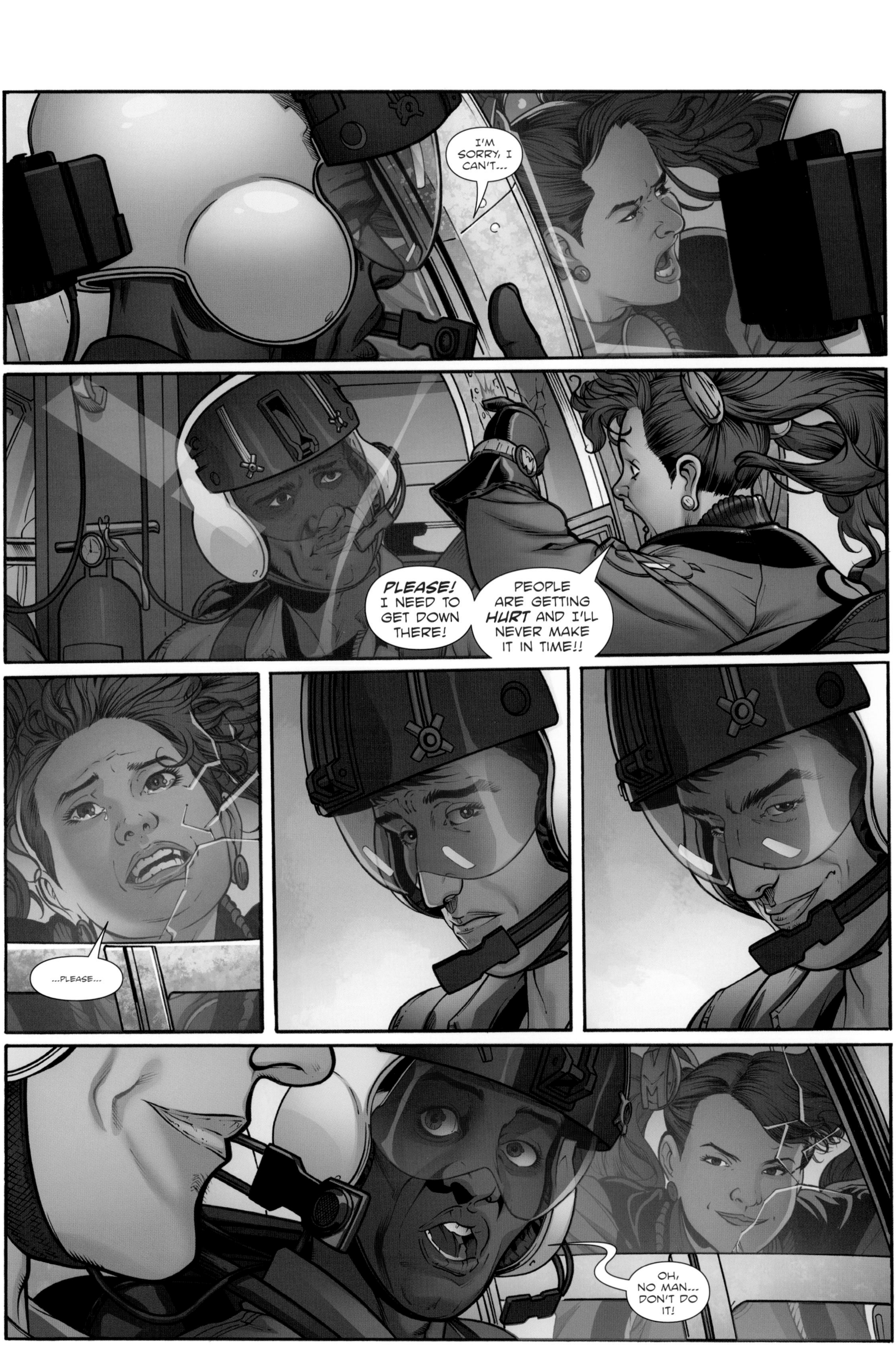
I'M SORRY, I CAN'T...
PLEASE! I NEED TO GET DOWN THERE!
PEOPLE ARE GETTING HURT AND I'LL NEVER MAKE IT IN TIME!!
...PLEASE...
OH, NO MAN... DON'T DO IT!

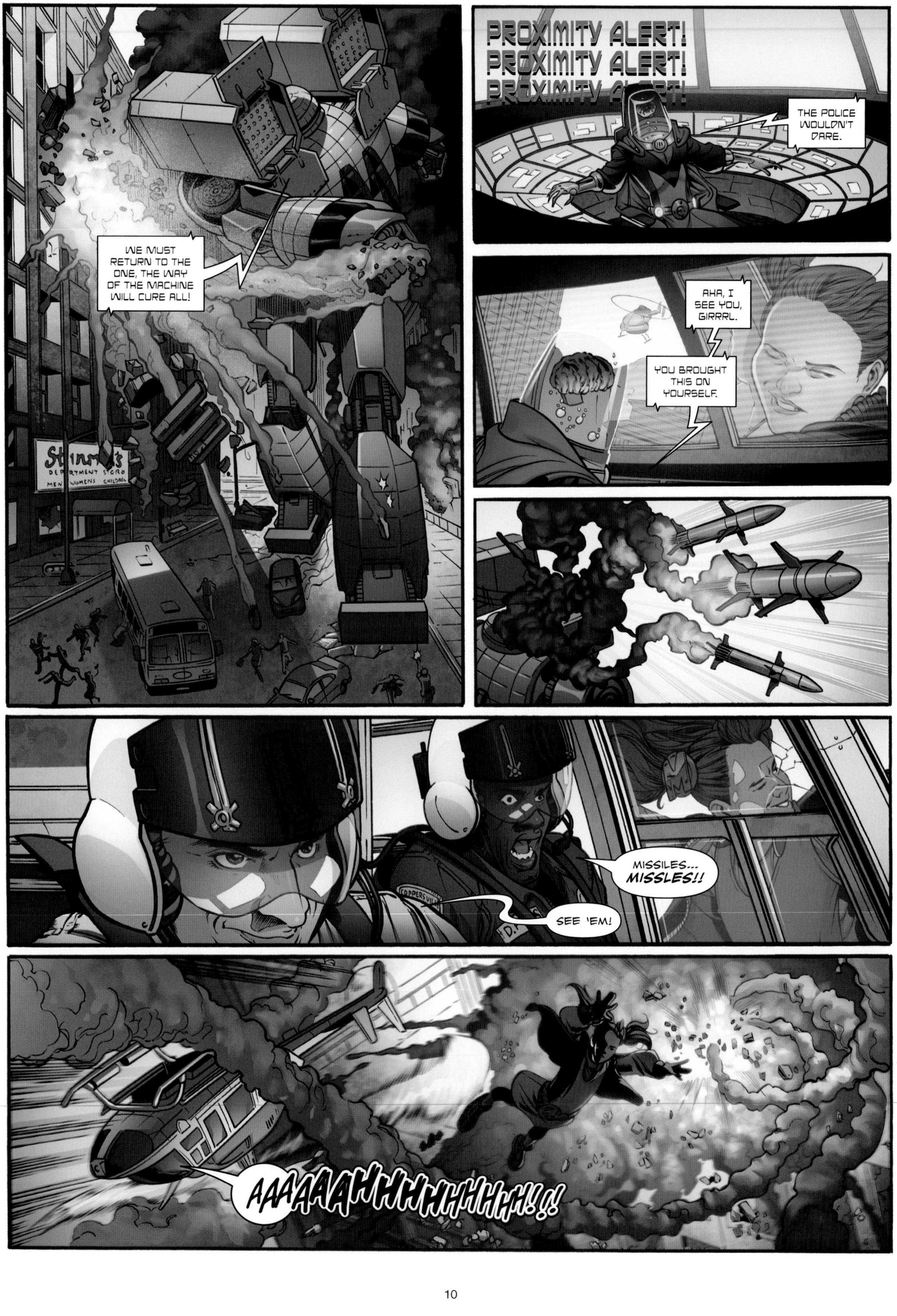

WE MUST RETURN TO THE ONE, THE WAY OF THE MACHINE WILL CURE ALL!
PROXIMITY ALERT! PROXIMITY ALERT! PROXIMITY ALERT!
THE POLICE WOULDN'T DARE.
AHA, I SEE YOU, GIRRRL.
YOU BROUGHT THIS ON YOURSELF.
MISSILES... MISSLES!!
SEE 'EM!
AAAAAAHHHHHHHHHH!!!

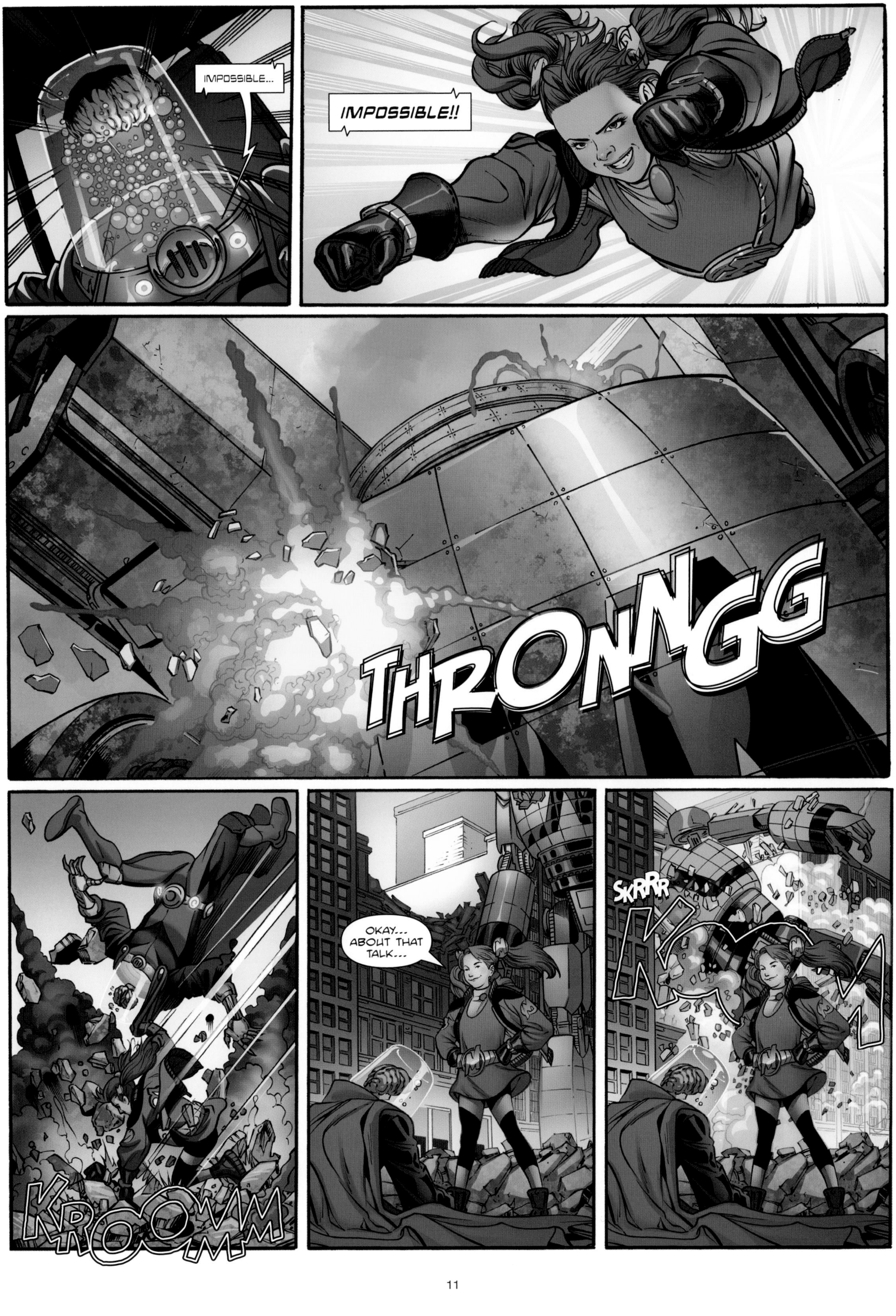
IMPOSSIBLE...
IMPOSSIBLE!!
THRONNGG
KROOMM
OKAY... ABOUT THAT TALK...
SKRRR

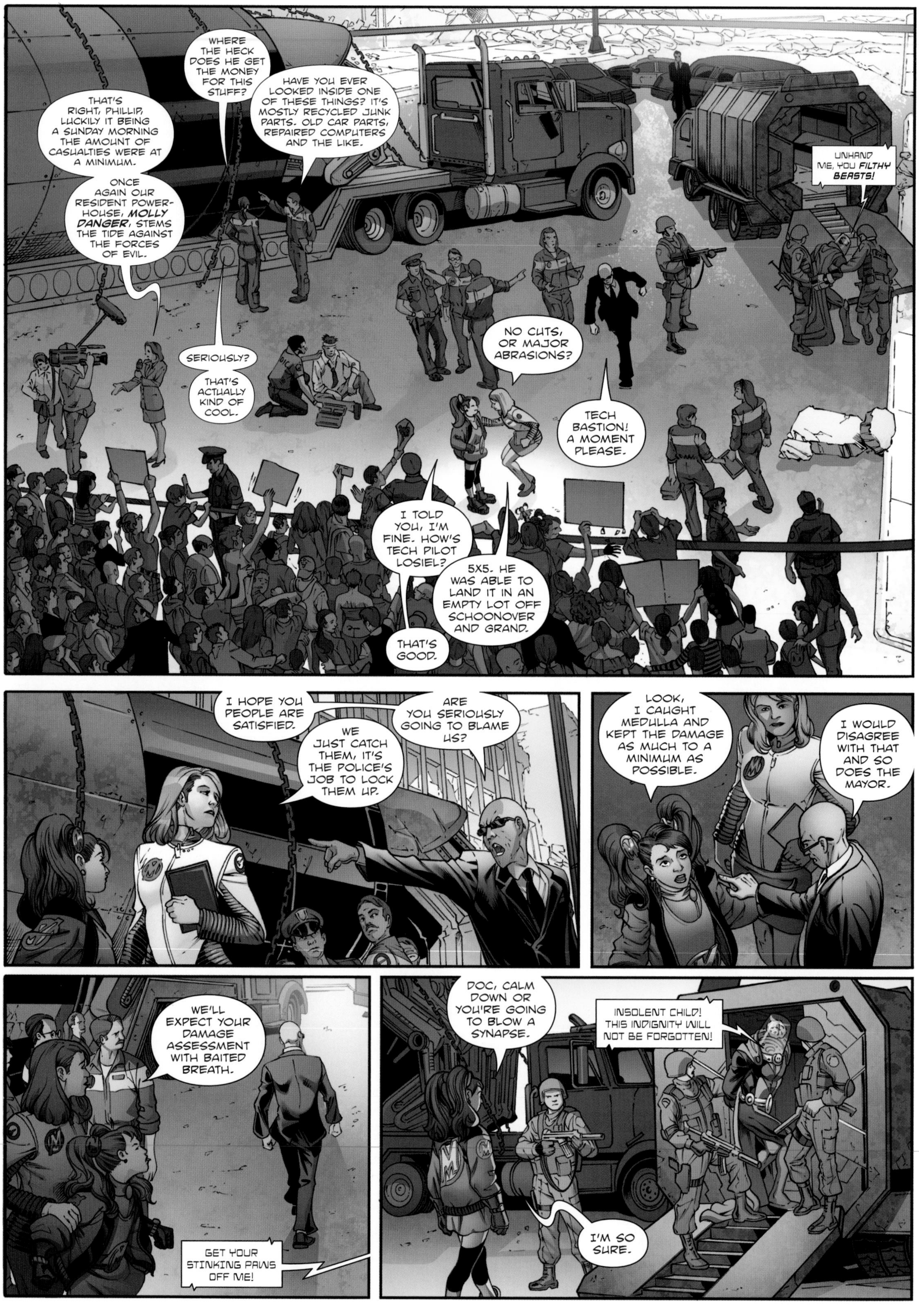
THAT'S RIGHT, PHILLIP, LUCKILY IT BEING A SUNDAY MORNING THE AMOUNT OF CASUALTIES WERE AT A MINIMUM.
ONCE AGAIN OUR RESIDENT POWER-HOUSE, MOLLY DANGER, STEMS THE TIDE AGAINST THE FORCES OF EVIL.
WHERE THE HECK DOES HE GET THE MONEY FOR THIS STUFF?
HAVE YOU EVER LOOKED INSIDE ONE OF THESE THINGS? IT'S MOSTLY RECYCLED JUNK PARTS. OLD CAR PARTS, REPAIRED COMPUTERS AND THE LIKE.
SERIOUSLY?
THAT'S ACTUALLY KIND OF COOL.
UNHAND ME, YOU FILTHY BEASTS!
NO CUTS, OR MAJOR ABRASIONS?
TECH BASTION! A MOMENT PLEASE.
I TOLD YOU, I'M FINE. HOW'S TECH PILOT LOSIEL?
5X5. HE WAS ABLE TO LAND IT IN AN EMPTY LOT OFF SCHOONOVER AND GRAND.
THAT'S GOOD.
I HOPE YOU PEOPLE ARE SATISFIED.
WE JUST CATCH THEM, IT'S THE POLICE'S JOB TO LOCK THEM UP.
ARE YOU SERIOUSLY GOING TO BLAME US?
LOOK, I CAUGHT MEDULLA AND KEPT THE DAMAGE AS MUCH TO A MINIMUM AS POSSIBLE.
I WOULD DISAGREE WITH THAT AND SO DOES THE MAYOR.
WE'LL EXPECT YOUR DAMAGE ASSESSMENT WITH BAITED BREATH.
GET YOUR STINKING PAWS OFF ME!
DOC, CALM DOWN OR YOU'RE GOING TO BLOW A SYNAPSE.
INSOLENT CHILD! THIS INDIGNITY WILL NOT BE FORGOTTEN!
I'M SO SURE.

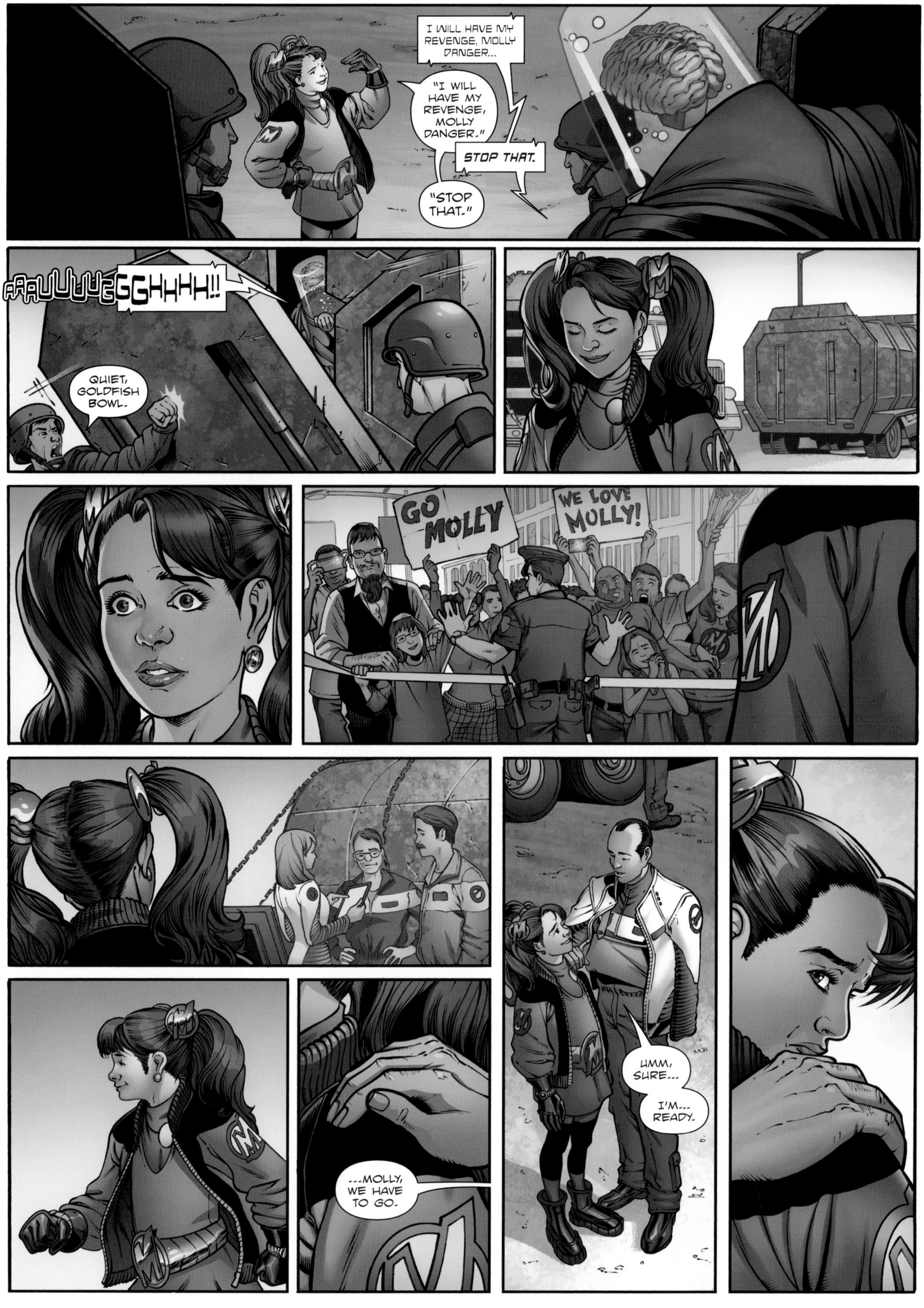
I WILL HAVE MY REVENGE, MOLLY DANGER...
"I WILL HAVE MY REVENGE, MOLLY DANGER."
STOP THAT.
"STOP THAT."
AAAUUUUGGHHHH!!
QUIET, GOLDFISH BOWL.
GO MOLLY
WE LOVE MOLLY!
UMM, SURE...
I'M... READY.
...MOLLY, WE HAVE TO GO.

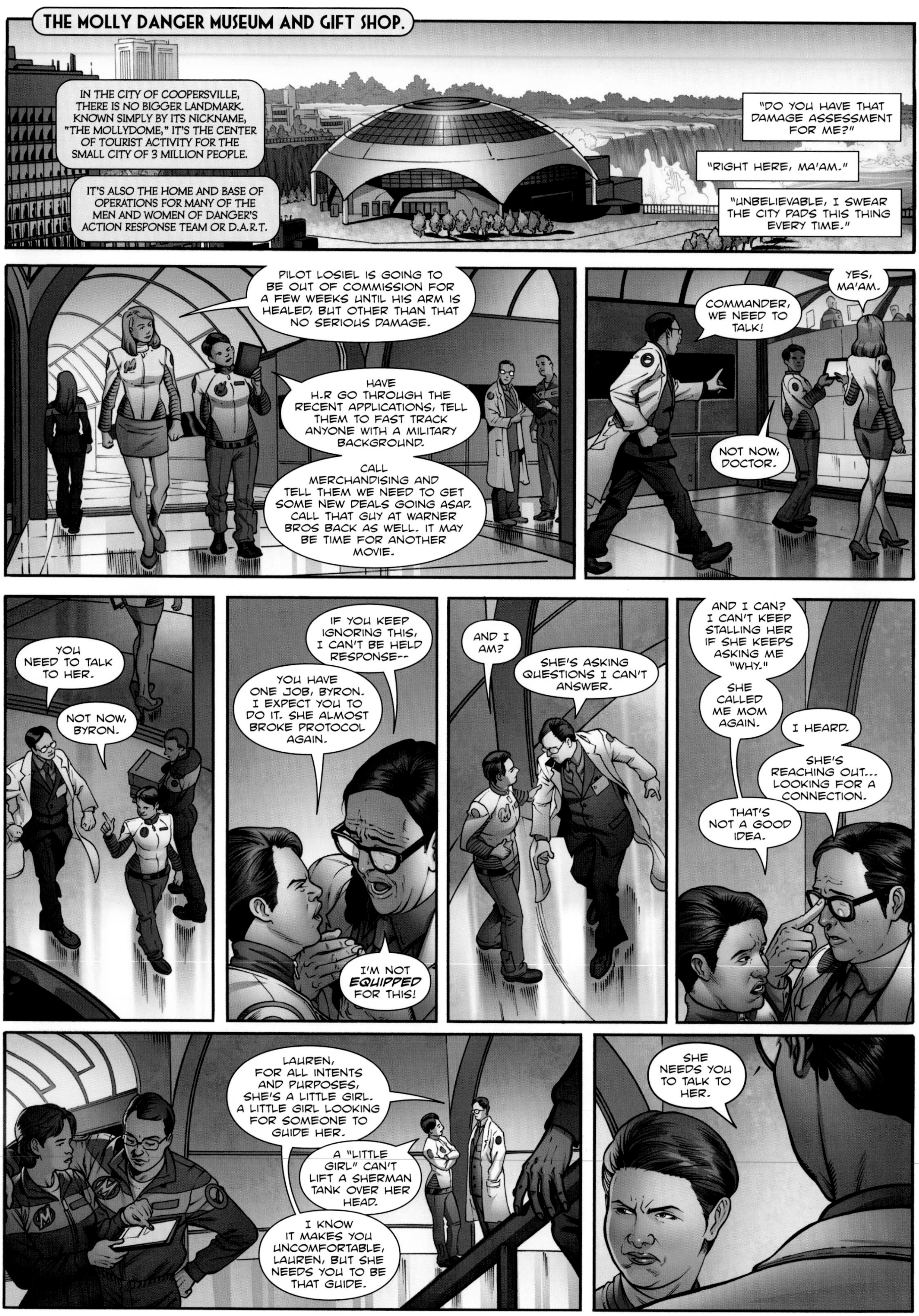
THE MOLLY DANGER MUSEUM AND GIFT SHOP.
IN THE CITY OF COOPERSVILLE, THERE IS NO BIGGER LANDMARK. KNOWN SIMPLY BY ITS NICKNAME, "THE MOLLYDOME," IT'S THE CENTER OF TOURIST ACTIVITY FOR THE SMALL CITY OF 3 MILLION PEOPLE.
IT'S ALSO THE HOME AND BASE OF OPERATIONS FOR MANY OF THE MEN AND WOMEN OF DANGER'S ACTION RESPONSE TEAM OR D.A.R.T.
"DO YOU HAVE THAT DAMAGE ASSESSMENT FOR ME?"
"RIGHT HERE, MA'AM."
"UNBELIEVABLE, I SWEAR THE CITY PADS THIS THING EVERY TIME."
PILOT LOSIEL IS GOING TO BE OUT OF COMMISSION FOR A FEW WEEKS UNTIL HIS ARM IS HEALED, BUT OTHER THAN THAT NO SERIOUS DAMAGE.
HAVE H.R GO THROUGH THE RECENT APPLICATIONS, TELL THEM TO FAST TRACK ANYONE WITH A MILITARY BACKGROUND.
CALL MERCHANDISING AND TELL THEM WE NEED TO GET SOME NEW DEALS GOING ASAP. CALL THAT GUY AT WARNER BROS BACK AS WELL. IT MAY BE TIME FOR ANOTHER MOVIE.
YES, MA'AM.
COMMANDER, WE NEED TO TALK!
NOT NOW, DOCTOR.
YOU NEED TO TALK TO HER.
NOT NOW, BYRON.
IF YOU KEEP IGNORING THIS, I CAN'T BE HELD RESPONSE--
YOU HAVE ONE JOB, BYRON. I EXPECT YOU TO DO IT. SHE ALMOST BROKE PROTOCOL AGAIN.
I'M NOT *EQUIPPED* FOR THIS!
AND I AM?
SHE'S ASKING QUESTIONS I CAN'T ANSWER.
AND I CAN? I CAN'T KEEP STALLING HER IF SHE KEEPS ASKING ME "WHY."
SHE CALLED ME MOM AGAIN.
I HEARD.
SHE'S REACHING OUT... LOOKING FOR A CONNECTION.
THAT'S NOT A GOOD IDEA.
LAUREN, FOR ALL INTENTS AND PURPOSES, SHE'S A LITTLE GIRL. A LITTLE GIRL LOOKING FOR SOMEONE TO GUIDE HER.
A "LITTLE GIRL" CAN'T LIFT A SHERMAN TANK OVER HER HEAD.
I KNOW IT MAKES YOU UNCOMFORTABLE, LAUREN, BUT SHE NEEDS YOU TO BE THAT GUIDE.
SHE NEEDS YOU TO TALK TO HER.

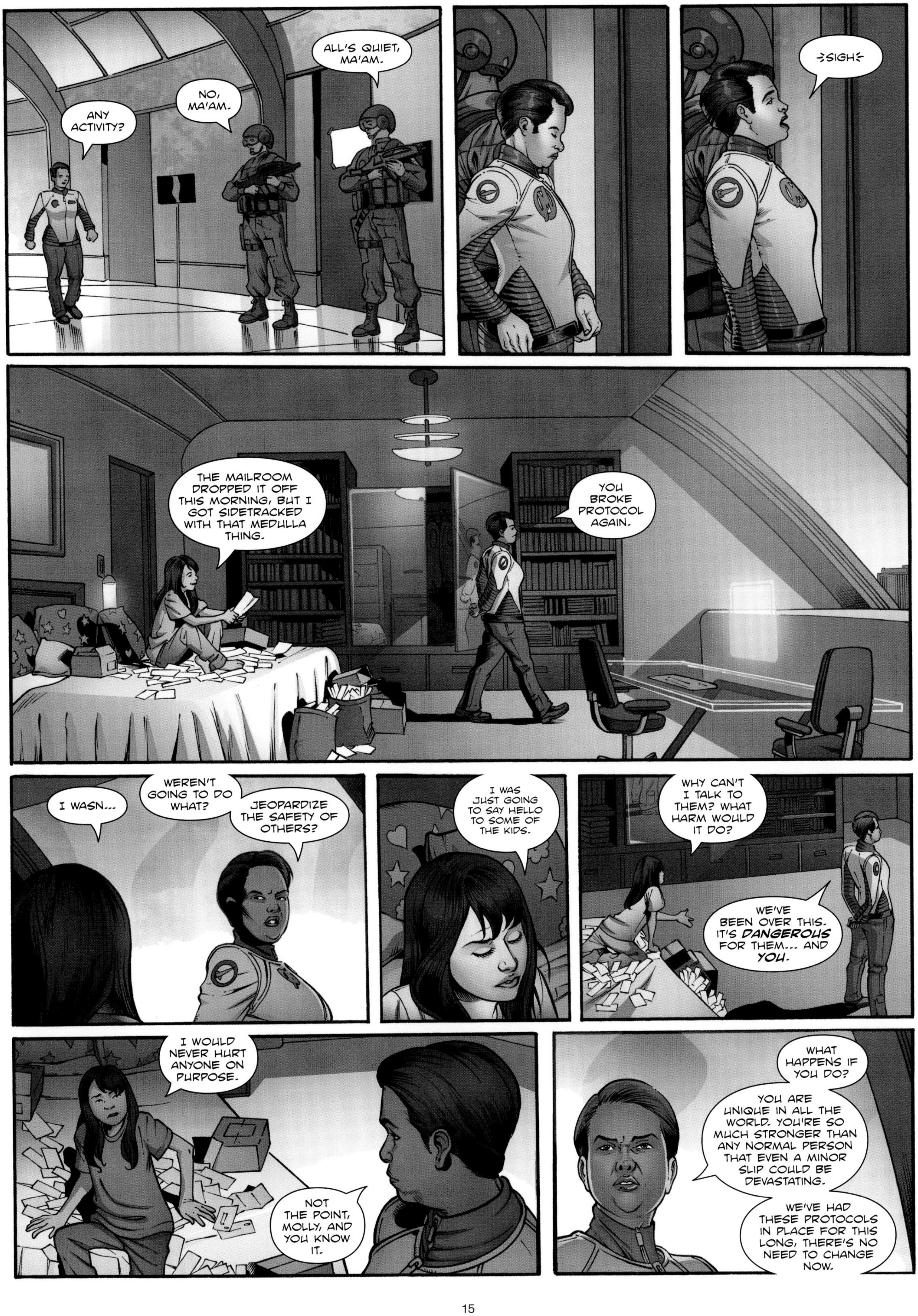
ANY ACTIVITY?
NO, MA'AM.
ALL'S QUIET, MA'AM.
SIGH
THE MAILROOM DROPPED IT OFF THIS MORNING, BUT I GOT SIDETRACKED WITH THAT MEDULLA THING.
YOU BROKE PROTOCOL AGAIN.
I WASN...
WEREN'T GOING TO DO WHAT?
JEOPARDIZE THE SAFETY OF OTHERS?
I WAS JUST GOING TO SAY HELLO TO SOME OF THE KIDS.
WHY CAN'T I TALK TO THEM? WHAT HARM WOULD IT DO?
WE'VE BEEN OVER THIS. IT'S DANGEROUS FOR THEM... AND YOU.
I WOULD NEVER HURT ANYONE ON PURPOSE.
NOT THE POINT, MOLLY, AND YOU KNOW IT.
WHAT HAPPENS IF YOU DO?
YOU ARE UNIQUE IN ALL THE WORLD. YOU'RE SO MUCH STRONGER THAN ANY NORMAL PERSON THAT EVEN A MINOR SLIP COULD BE DEVASTATING.
WE'VE HAD THESE PROTOCOLS IN PLACE FOR THIS LONG, THERE'S NO NEED TO CHANGE NOW.

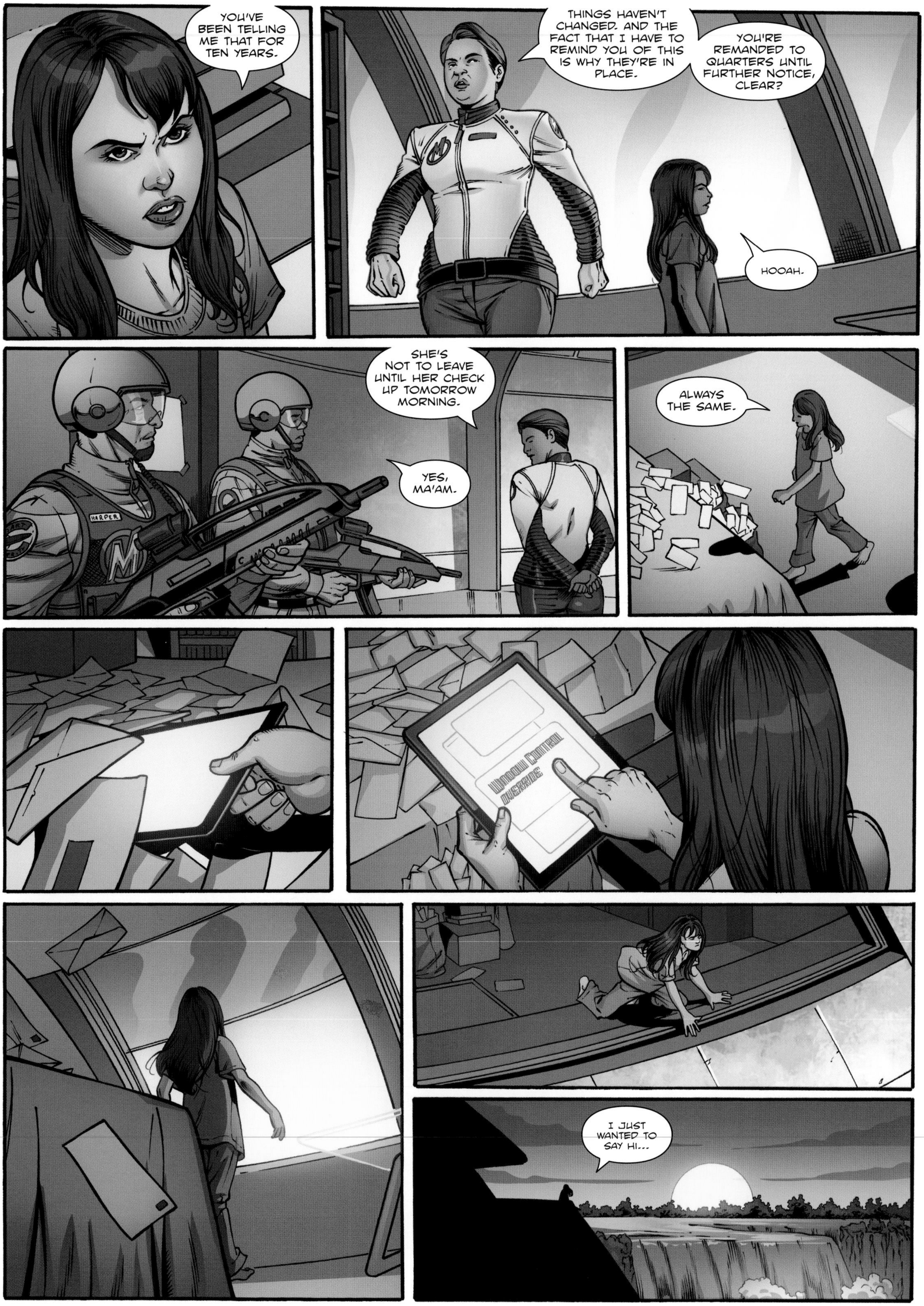
YOU'VE BEEN TELLING ME THAT FOR TEN YEARS.
THINGS HAVEN'T CHANGED. AND THE FACT THAT I HAVE TO REMIND YOU OF THIS IS WHY THEY'RE IN PLACE.
YOU'RE REMANDED TO QUARTERS UNTIL FURTHER NOTICE, CLEAR?
HOOAH.
SHE'S NOT TO LEAVE UNTIL HER CHECK UP TOMORROW MORNING.
YES, MA'AM.
HARPER
ALWAYS THE SAME.
Window Control Override
I JUST WANTED TO SAY HI...

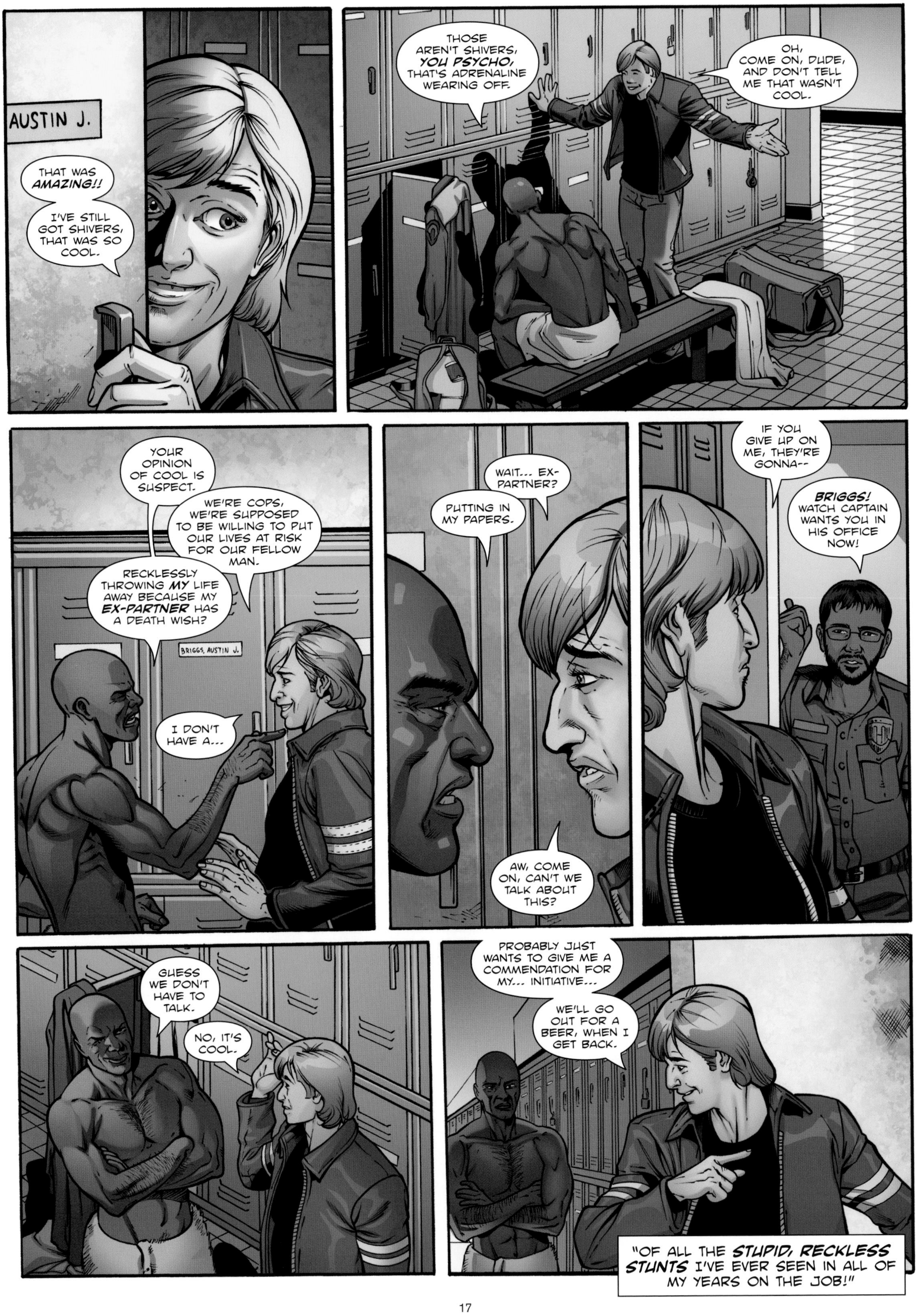
AUSTIN J.
THAT WAS AMAZING!!
I'VE STILL GOT SHIVERS, THAT WAS SO COOL.
THOSE AREN'T SHIVERS, YOU PSYCHO, THAT'S ADRENALINE WEARING OFF.
OH, COME ON, DUDE, AND DON'T TELL ME THAT WASN'T COOL.
YOUR OPINION OF COOL IS SUSPECT.
WE'RE COPS, WE'RE SUPPOSED TO BE WILLING TO PUT OUR LIVES AT RISK FOR OUR FELLOW MAN.
RECKLESSLY THROWING MY LIFE AWAY BECAUSE MY EX-PARTNER HAS A DEATH WISH?
BRIGGS, AUSTIN J.
I DON'T HAVE A...
PUTTING IN MY PAPERS.
WAIT... EX-PARTNER?
AW, COME ON, CAN'T WE TALK ABOUT THIS?
IF YOU GIVE UP ON ME, THEY'RE GONNA--
BRIGGS! WATCH CAPTAIN WANTS YOU IN HIS OFFICE NOW!
GUESS WE DON'T HAVE TO TALK.
NO, IT'S COOL.
PROBABLY JUST WANTS TO GIVE ME A COMMENDATION FOR MY... INITIATIVE...
WE'LL GO OUT FOR A BEER, WHEN I GET BACK.
"OF ALL THE STUPID, RECKLESS STUNTS I'VE EVER SEEN IN ALL OF MY YEARS ON THE JOB!"

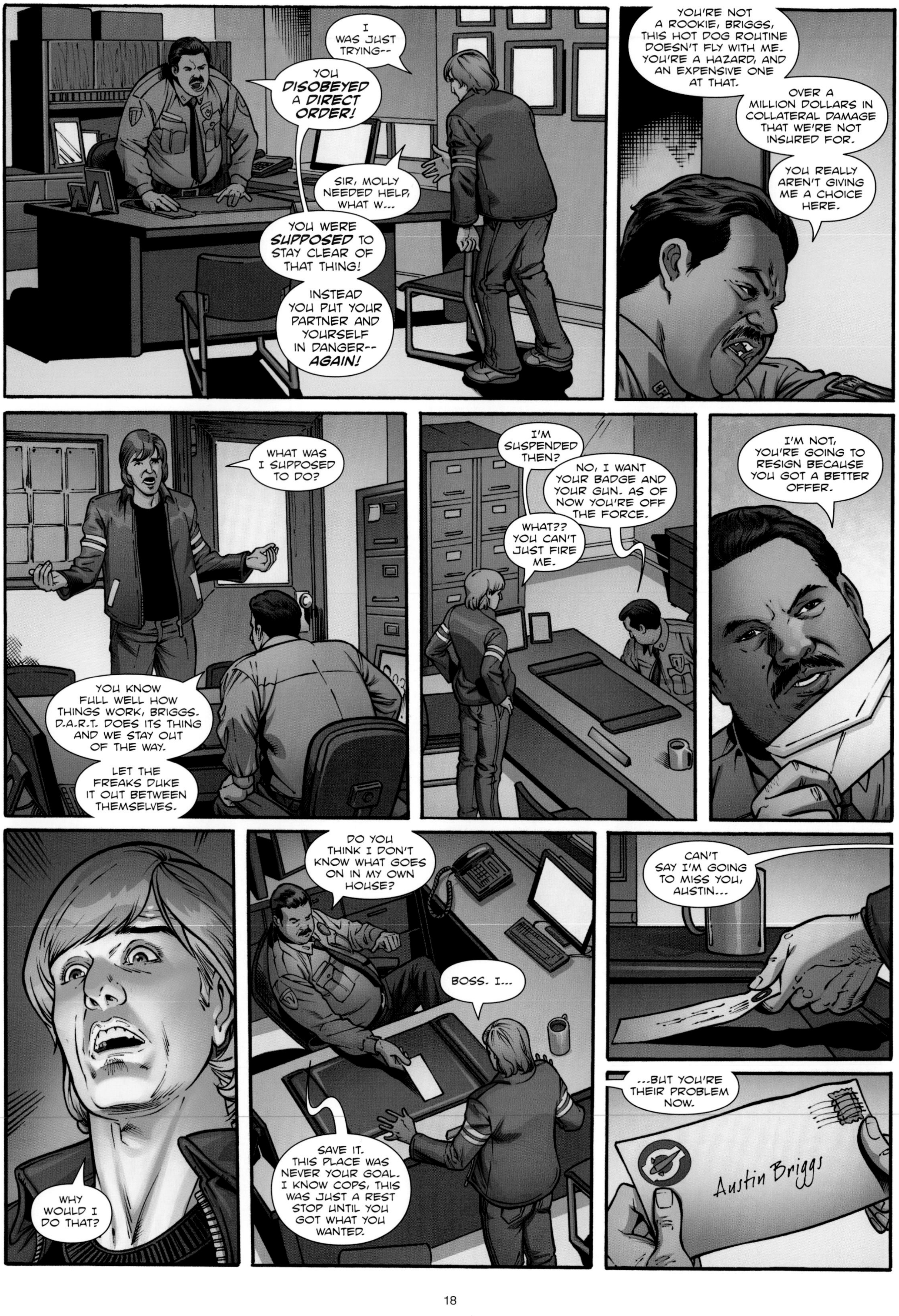

I WAS JUST TRYING--
YOU DISOBEYED A DIRECT ORDER!
SIR, MOLLY NEEDED HELP, WHAT W...
YOU WERE SUPPOSED TO STAY CLEAR OF THAT THING!
INSTEAD YOU PUT YOUR PARTNER AND YOURSELF IN DANGER-- AGAIN!
YOU'RE NOT A ROOKIE, BRIGGS, THIS HOT DOG ROUTINE DOESN'T FLY WITH ME. YOU'RE A HAZARD, AND AN EXPENSIVE ONE AT THAT.
OVER A MILLION DOLLARS IN COLLATERAL DAMAGE THAT WE'RE NOT INSURED FOR.
YOU REALLY AREN'T GIVING ME A CHOICE HERE.
WHAT WAS I SUPPOSED TO DO?
YOU KNOW FULL WELL HOW THINGS WORK, BRIGGS. D.A.R.T. DOES ITS THING AND WE STAY OUT OF THE WAY.
LET THE FREAKS DUKE IT OUT BETWEEN THEMSELVES.
I'M SUSPENDED THEN?
NO, I WANT YOUR BADGE AND YOUR GUN. AS OF NOW YOU'RE OFF THE FORCE.
WHAT?? YOU CAN'T JUST FIRE ME.
I'M NOT, YOU'RE GOING TO RESIGN BECAUSE YOU GOT A BETTER OFFER.
WHY WOULD I DO THAT?
DO YOU THINK I DON'T KNOW WHAT GOES ON IN MY OWN HOUSE?
BOSS. I...
SAVE IT. THIS PLACE WAS NEVER YOUR GOAL. I KNOW COPS, THIS WAS JUST A REST STOP UNTIL YOU GOT WHAT YOU WANTED.
CAN'T SAY I'M GOING TO MISS YOU, AUSTIN...
...BUT YOU'RE THEIR PROBLEM NOW.
Austin Briggs

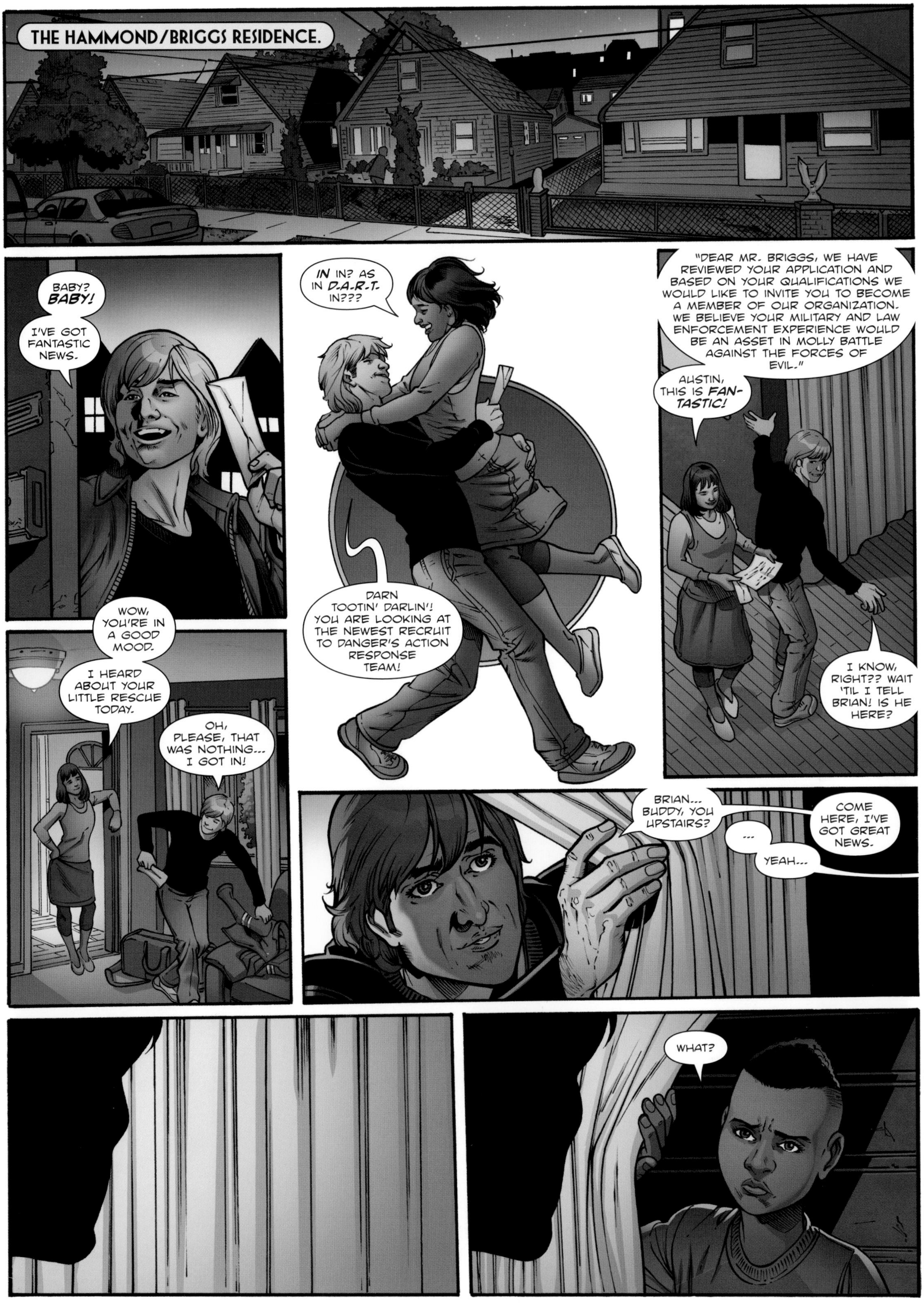
THE HAMMOND/BRIGGS RESIDENCE.
BABY? BABY!
I'VE GOT FANTASTIC NEWS.
IN IN? AS IN D.A.R.T. IN???
DARN TOOTIN' DARLIN'! YOU ARE LOOKING AT THE NEWEST RECRUIT TO DANGER'S ACTION RESPONSE TEAM!
"DEAR MR. BRIGGS, WE HAVE REVIEWED YOUR APPLICATION AND BASED ON YOUR QUALIFICATIONS WE WOULD LIKE TO INVITE YOU TO BECOME A MEMBER OF OUR ORGANIZATION. WE BELIEVE YOUR MILITARY AND LAW ENFORCEMENT EXPERIENCE WOULD BE AN ASSET IN MOLLY BATTLE AGAINST THE FORCES OF EVIL."
AUSTIN, THIS IS FANTASTIC!
I KNOW, RIGHT?? WAIT 'TIL I TELL BRIAN! IS HE HERE?
WOW, YOU'RE IN A GOOD MOOD.
I HEARD ABOUT YOUR LITTLE RESCUE TODAY.
OH, PLEASE, THAT WAS NOTHING... I GOT IN!
BRIAN... BUDDY, YOU UPSTAIRS?
...
COME HERE, I'VE GOT GREAT NEWS.
YEAH...
WHAT?

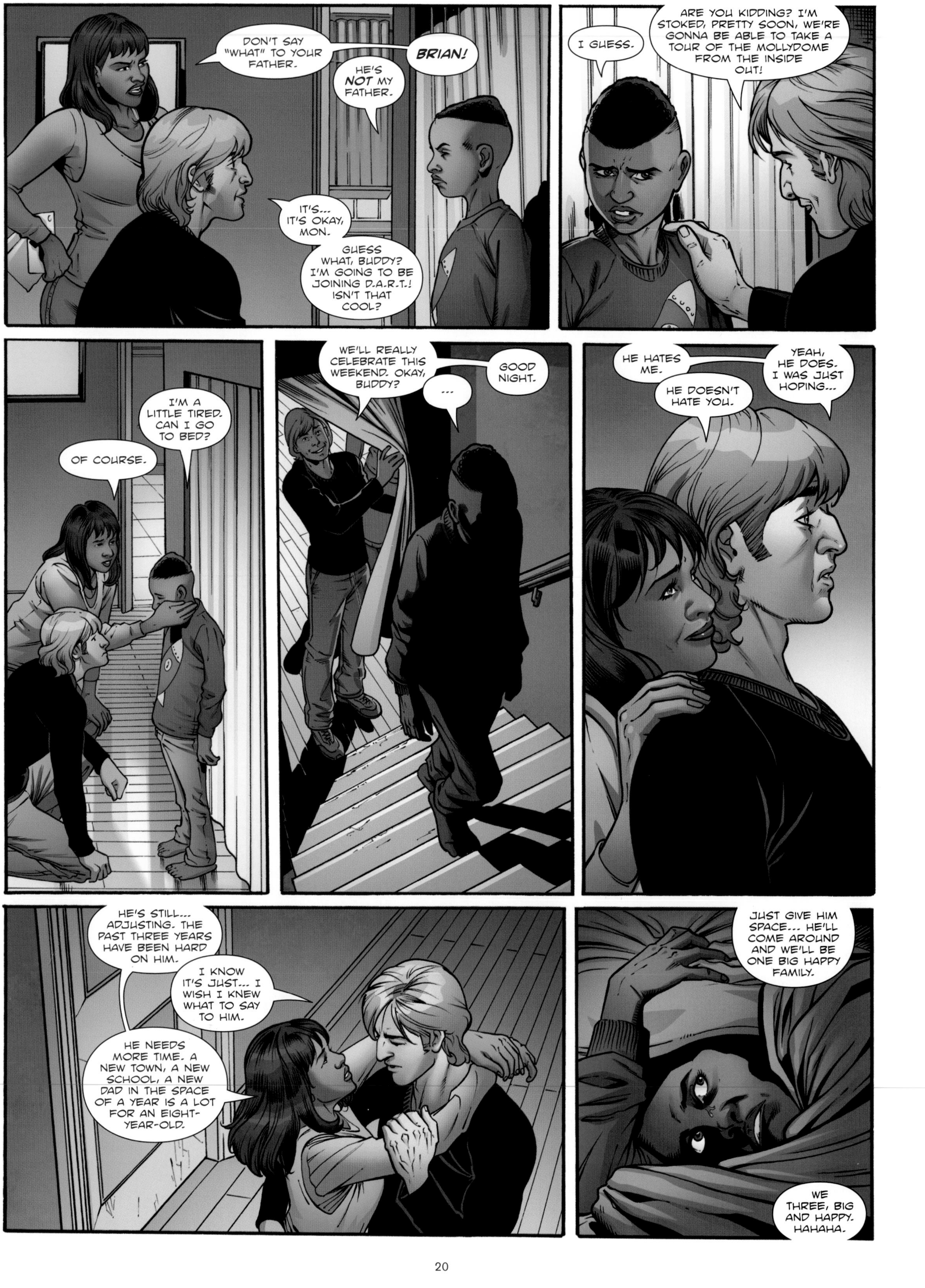

DON'T SAY "WHAT" TO YOUR FATHER.
BRIAN!
HE'S NOT MY FATHER.
IT'S... IT'S OKAY, MON.
GUESS WHAT, BUDDY? I'M GOING TO BE JOINING D.A.R.T.! ISN'T THAT COOL?
I GUESS.
ARE YOU KIDDING? I'M STOKED, PRETTY SOON, WE'RE GONNA BE ABLE TO TAKE A TOUR OF THE MOLLYDOME FROM THE INSIDE OUT!
I'M A LITTLE TIRED. CAN I GO TO BED?
OF COURSE.
WE'LL REALLY CELEBRATE THIS WEEKEND. OKAY, BUDDY?
...
GOOD NIGHT.
HE HATES ME.
HE DOESN'T HATE YOU.
YEAH, HE DOES. I WAS JUST HOPING...
HE'S STILL... ADJUSTING. THE PAST THREE YEARS HAVE BEEN HARD ON HIM.
I KNOW IT'S JUST... I WISH I KNEW WHAT TO SAY TO HIM.
HE NEEDS MORE TIME. A NEW TOWN, A NEW SCHOOL, A NEW DAD IN THE SPACE OF A YEAR IS A LOT FOR AN EIGHT-YEAR-OLD.
JUST GIVE HIM SPACE... HE'LL COME AROUND AND WE'LL BE ONE BIG HAPPY FAMILY.
WE THREE, BIG AND HAPPY. HAHAHA.

"OKAY, EVERYONE, EYES ON ME, PLEASE.

"MA'AM? MA'AM? COULD YOU... THANK YOU.

"OKAY, CAN EVERYONE HEAR ME? GOOD. HI, I'M CAMERON AND I'D LIKE TO WELCOME YOU TO THE MOLLY DANGER MUSEUM."

AUSTIN BRIGGS?

THAT'S ME. I MEAN, YES, MA'AM.

SO WHO CAN TELL ME WHAT THEY KNOW ABOUT MOLLY?

YES, HOW ABOUT YOU?

MOLLY'S AN ALIEN FROM A PLANET CALLED GAMMA 7.

YES, VERY GOOD. MOLLY'S FAMILY WERE PART OF A GROUP OF COLONISTS AND SCIENTISTS FROM A WORLD MOLLY TELLS US WAS PART OF THE "GREAT GALACTIC RIM."

NO NEED TO BE FORMAL, AUSTIN. I'M EMMA BASTION, D.A.R.T. SECURITY LIAISON.

I'M SORRY, BUT WHAT'S THE GALACTIC RIM?

IT'S A STAR SYSTEM OF MANY WORLDS ON THE FAR SIDE OF THE SOLAR SYSTEM. MOLLY'S HOME WORLD WAS PART OF THE GAMMA CLUSTER.

FOLLOW ME, PLEASE.

MOLLY'S PEOPLE WERE ON THEIR WAY TO EXPLORING AN UNCHARTED SECTOR OF OUR SOLAR SYSTEM WHEN SOME THING WENT WRONG.

WHAT HAPPENED?

I KNOW! I KNOW!

THEIR SHIP CRASHED ON EARTH INSTEAD OF WHERE THEY WERE HEADED AND ALMOST EVERYONE DIED EXCEPT HER.

THAT'S TRUE; MOLLY LOST BOTH HER PARENTS AND HER BROTHER. BUT WHAT HAPPENED NEXT WOULD CHANGE HER AND OUR WORLD FOREVER.

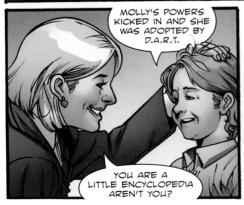

MOLLY'S POWERS KICKED IN AND SHE WAS ADOPTED BY D.A.R.T.

YOU ARE A LITTLE ENCYCLOPEDIA AREN'T YOU?

D.A.R.T. WAS ACTUALLY CREATED AFTER THE U.S. GOVERNMENT FOUND MOLLY'S SHIP IN THE ADIRONDACK MOUNTAINS TWENTY TWO YEARS AGO.

MOLLY SPENT NEARLY A YEAR IN A COMA BUT WHEN SHE AWOKE, WE DISCOVERED THAT THE COMA WAS ACTUALLY HER BODY'S SYSTEMS ALTERING THEMSELVES.

OUR ATMOSPHERE TRANSFORMED MOLLY, MAKING HER SUPERHUMANLY STRONG, INVULNERABLE TO HARM AND AS FAR AS WE KNOW..

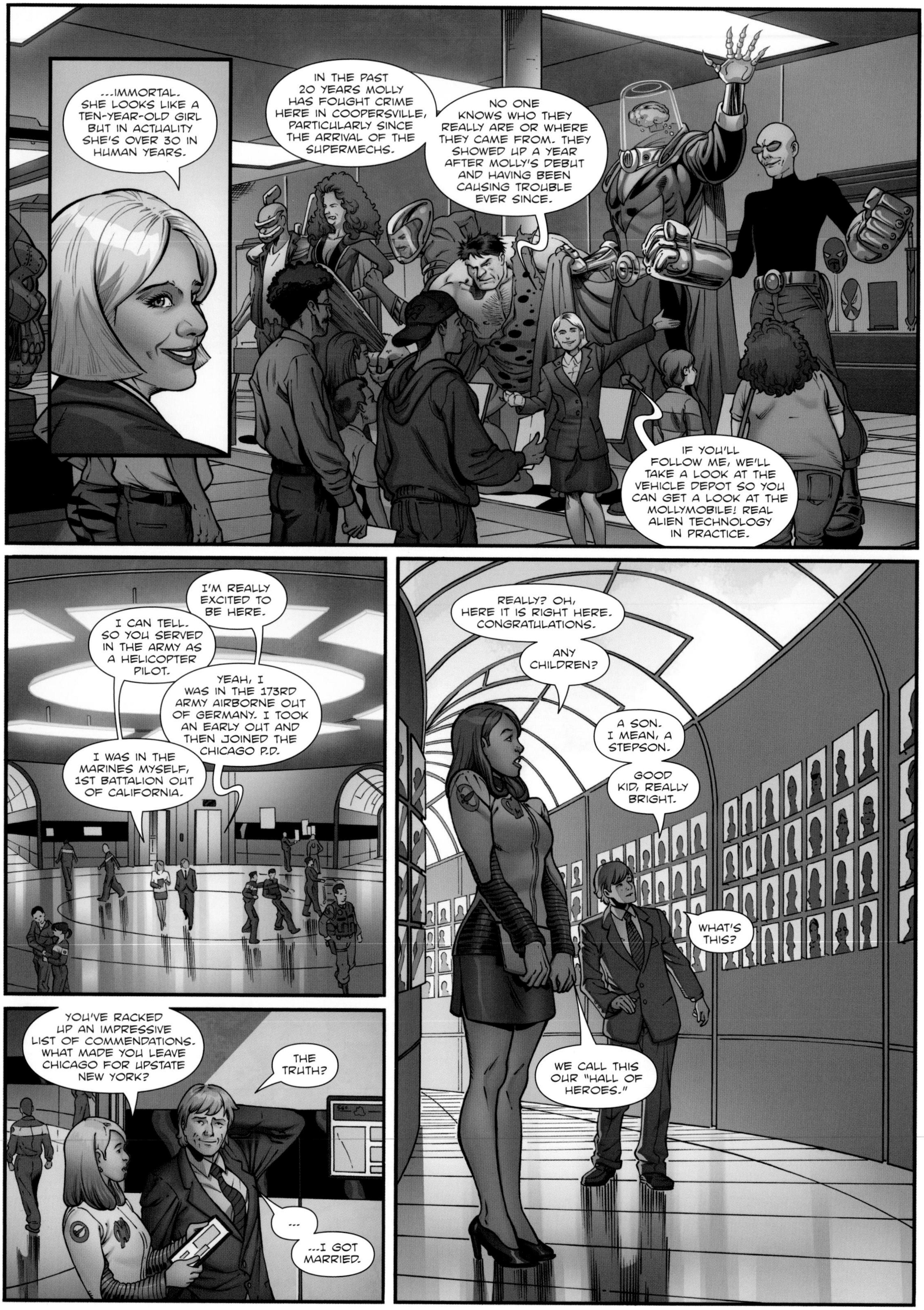
...IMMORTAL. SHE LOOKS LIKE A TEN-YEAR-OLD GIRL BUT IN ACTUALITY SHE'S OVER 30 IN HUMAN YEARS.
IN THE PAST 20 YEARS MOLLY HAS FOUGHT CRIME HERE IN COOPERSVILLE, PARTICULARLY SINCE THE ARRIVAL OF THE SUPERMECHS.
NO ONE KNOWS WHO THEY REALLY ARE OR WHERE THEY CAME FROM. THEY SHOWED UP A YEAR AFTER MOLLY'S DEBUT AND HAVING BEEN CAUSING TROUBLE EVER SINCE.
IF YOU'LL FOLLOW ME, WE'LL TAKE A LOOK AT THE VEHICLE DEPOT SO YOU CAN GET A LOOK AT THE MOLLYMOBILE! REAL ALIEN TECHNOLOGY IN PRACTICE.
I'M REALLY EXCITED TO BE HERE.
I CAN TELL. SO YOU SERVED IN THE ARMY AS A HELICOPTER PILOT.
YEAH, I WAS IN THE 173RD ARMY AIRBORNE OUT OF GERMANY. I TOOK AN EARLY OUT AND THEN JOINED THE CHICAGO P.D.
I WAS IN THE MARINES MYSELF, 1ST BATTALION OUT OF CALIFORNIA.
YOU'VE RACKED UP AN IMPRESSIVE LIST OF COMMENDATIONS. WHAT MADE YOU LEAVE CHICAGO FOR UPSTATE NEW YORK?
THE TRUTH?
...
...I GOT MARRIED.
REALLY? OH, HERE IT IS RIGHT HERE. CONGRATULATIONS.
ANY CHILDREN?
A SON. I MEAN, A STEPSON.
GOOD KID, REALLY BRIGHT.
WHAT'S THIS?
WE CALL THIS OUR "HALL OF HEROES."

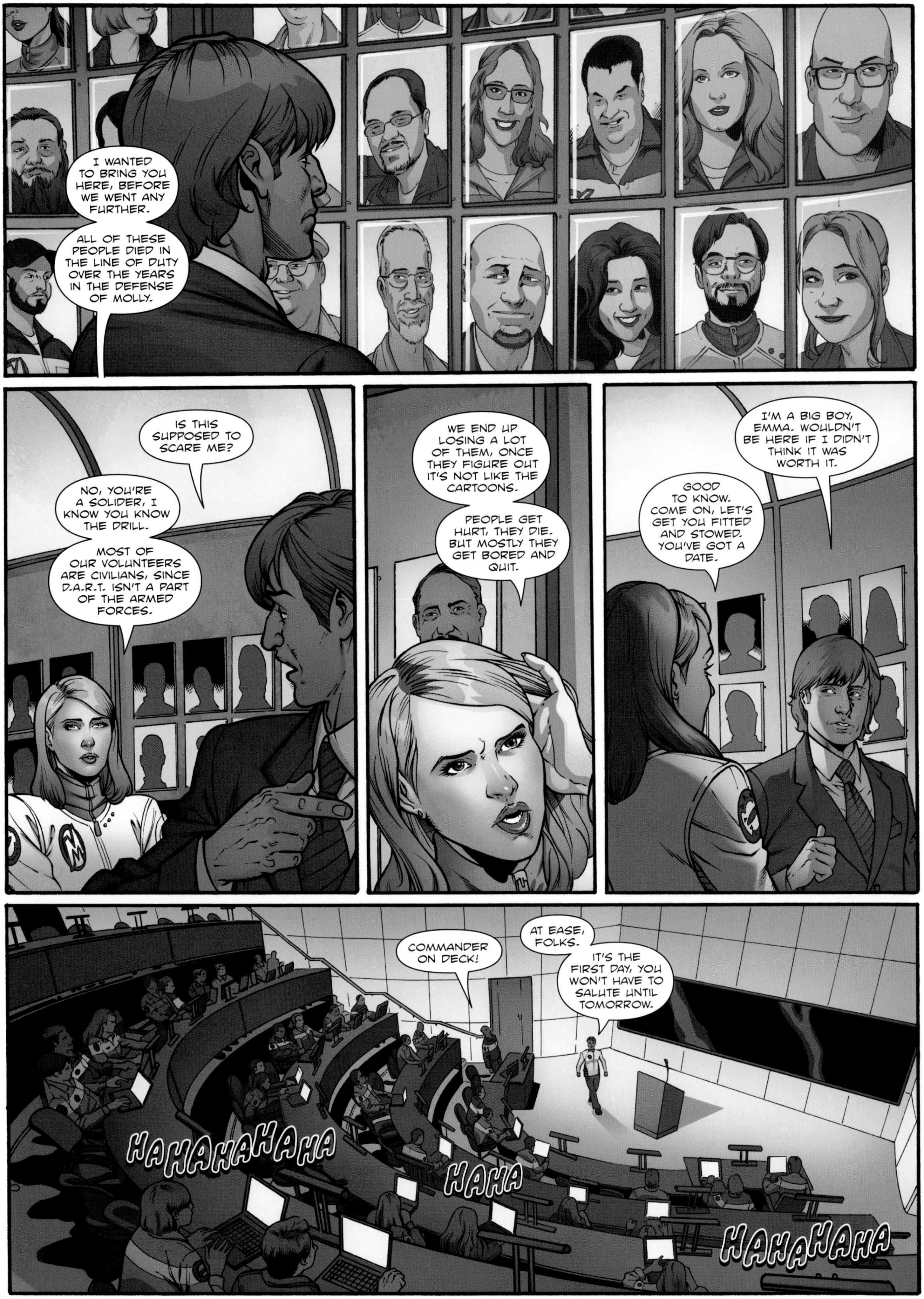

I WANTED TO BRING YOU HERE, BEFORE WE WENT ANY FURTHER.
ALL OF THESE PEOPLE DIED IN THE LINE OF DUTY OVER THE YEARS IN THE DEFENSE OF MOLLY.
IS THIS SUPPOSED TO SCARE ME?
NO, YOU'RE A SOLIDER, I KNOW YOU KNOW THE DRILL.
MOST OF OUR VOLUNTEERS ARE CIVILIANS, SINCE D.A.R.T. ISN'T A PART OF THE ARMED FORCES.
WE END UP LOSING A LOT OF THEM, ONCE THEY FIGURE OUT IT'S NOT LIKE THE CARTOONS.
PEOPLE GET HURT, THEY DIE. BUT MOSTLY THEY GET BORED AND QUIT.
I'M A BIG BOY, EMMA. WOULDN'T BE HERE IF I DIDN'T THINK IT WAS WORTH IT.
GOOD TO KNOW. COME ON, LET'S GET YOU FITTED AND STOWED. YOU'VE GOT A DATE.
COMMANDER ON DECK!
AT EASE, FOLKS.
IT'S THE FIRST DAY, YOU WON'T HAVE TO SALUTE UNTIL TOMORROW.
HAHAHAHAHAHA
HAHA
HAHAHAHAHA

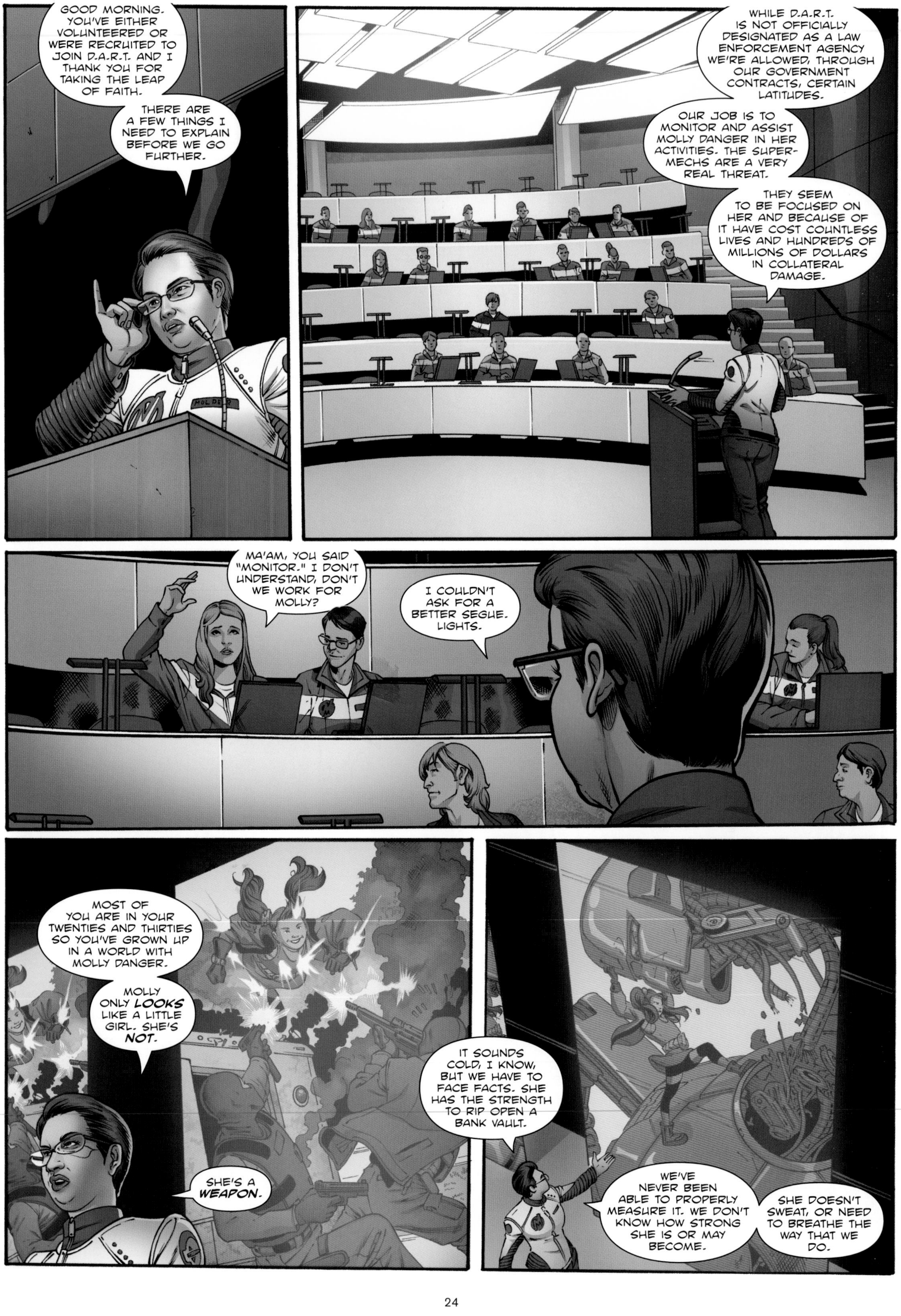
GOOD MORNING. YOU'VE EITHER VOLUNTEERED OR WERE RECRUITED TO JOIN D.A.R.T. AND I THANK YOU FOR TAKING THE LEAP OF FAITH.
THERE ARE A FEW THINGS I NEED TO EXPLAIN BEFORE WE GO FURTHER.
WHILE D.A.R.T. IS NOT OFFICIALLY DESIGNATED AS A LAW ENFORCEMENT AGENCY WE'RE ALLOWED, THROUGH OUR GOVERNMENT CONTRACTS, CERTAIN LATITUDES.
OUR JOB IS TO MONITOR AND ASSIST MOLLY DANGER IN HER ACTIVITIES. THE SUPER-MECHS ARE A VERY REAL THREAT.
THEY SEEM TO BE FOCUSED ON HER AND BECAUSE OF IT HAVE COST COUNTLESS LIVES AND HUNDREDS OF MILLIONS OF DOLLARS IN COLLATERAL DAMAGE.
MA'AM, YOU SAID "MONITOR." I DON'T UNDERSTAND, DON'T WE WORK FOR MOLLY?
I COULDN'T ASK FOR A BETTER SEGUE. LIGHTS.
MOST OF YOU ARE IN YOUR TWENTIES AND THIRTIES SO YOU'VE GROWN UP IN A WORLD WITH MOLLY DANGER.
MOLLY ONLY **LOOKS** LIKE A LITTLE GIRL. SHE'S ***NOT***.
SHE'S A ***WEAPON***.
IT SOUNDS COLD, I KNOW, BUT WE HAVE TO FACE FACTS. SHE HAS THE STRENGTH TO RIP OPEN A BANK VAULT.
WE'VE NEVER BEEN ABLE TO PROPERLY MEASURE IT. WE DON'T KNOW HOW STRONG SHE IS OR MAY BECOME.
SHE DOESN'T SWEAT, OR NEED TO BREATHE THE WAY THAT WE DO.

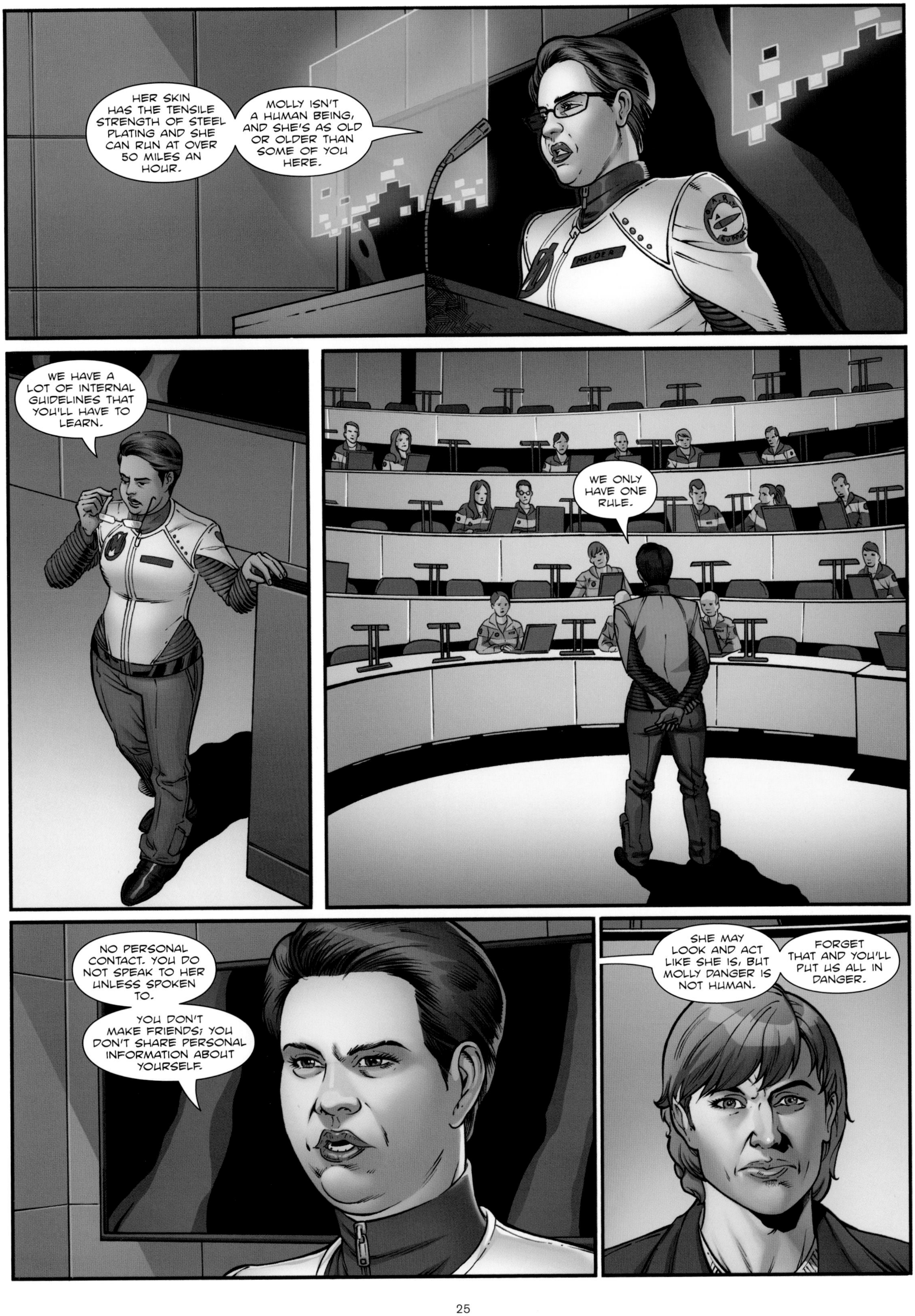
HER SKIN HAS THE TENSILE STRENGTH OF STEEL PLATING AND SHE CAN RUN AT OVER 50 MILES AN HOUR.
MOLLY ISN'T A HUMAN BEING, AND SHE'S AS OLD OR OLDER THAN SOME OF YOU HERE.
WE HAVE A LOT OF INTERNAL GUIDELINES THAT YOU'LL HAVE TO LEARN.
WE ONLY HAVE ONE RULE.
NO PERSONAL CONTACT. YOU DO NOT SPEAK TO HER UNLESS SPOKEN TO.
YOU DON'T MAKE FRIENDS; YOU DON'T SHARE PERSONAL INFORMATION ABOUT YOURSELF.
SHE MAY LOOK AND ACT LIKE SHE IS, BUT MOLLY DANGER IS NOT HUMAN.
FORGET THAT AND YOU'LL PUT US ALL IN DANGER.

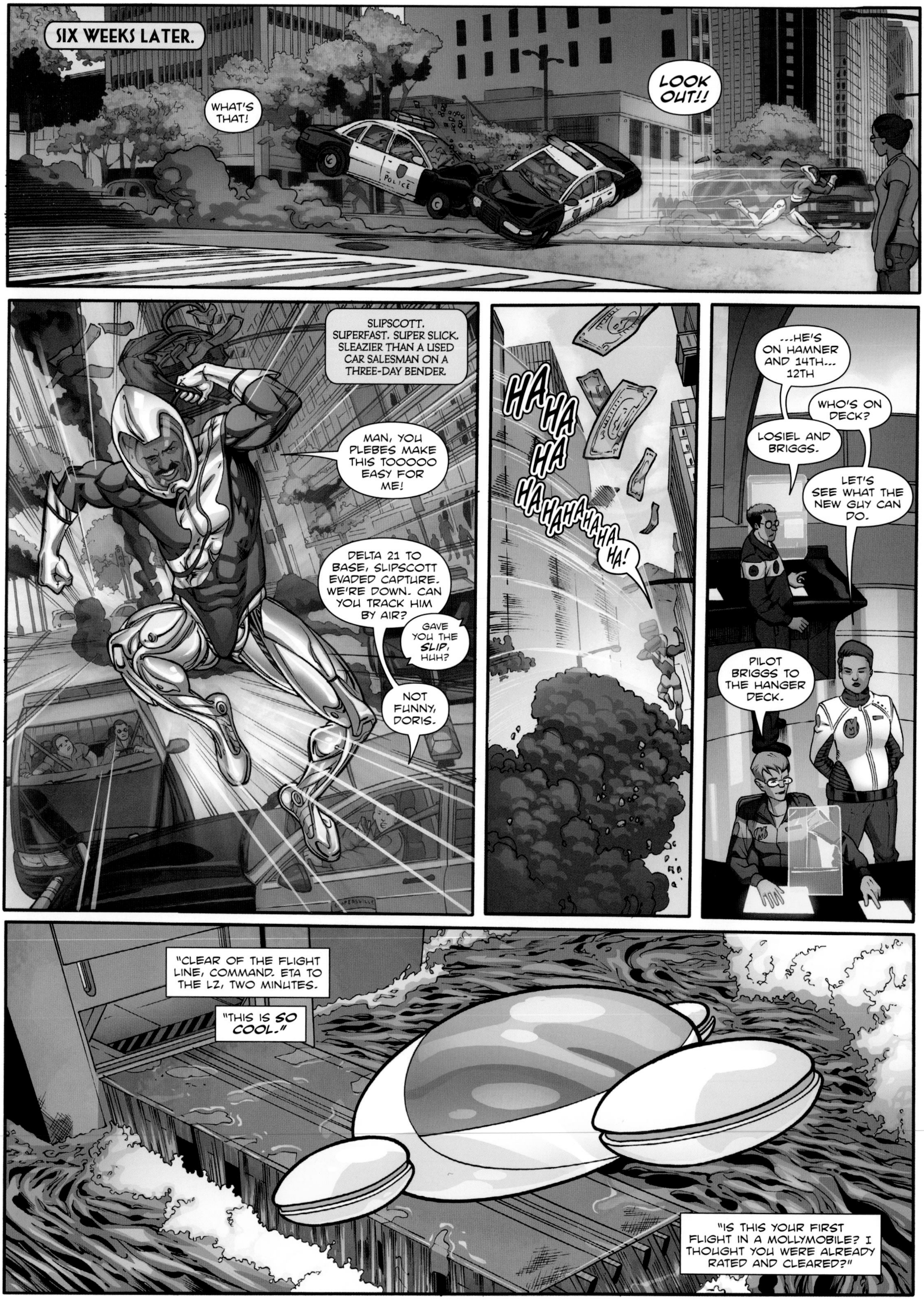

SIX WEEKS LATER.
WHAT'S THAT!
LOOK OUT!!
SLIPSCOTT. SUPERFAST. SUPER SLICK. SLEAZIER THAN A USED CAR SALESMAN ON A THREE-DAY BENDER.
MAN, YOU PLEBES MAKE THIS TOOOOO EASY FOR ME!
DELTA 21 TO BASE, SLIPSCOTT EVADED CAPTURE. WE'RE DOWN. CAN YOU TRACK HIM BY AIR?
GAVE YOU THE SLIP, HUH?
NOT FUNNY, DORIS.
HA HA HA HA HAHAHAHAHA!
...HE'S ON HAMNER AND 14TH... 12TH
WHO'S ON DECK?
LOSIEL AND BRIGGS.
LET'S SEE WHAT THE NEW GUY CAN DO.
PILOT BRIGGS TO THE HANGER DECK.
"CLEAR OF THE FLIGHT LINE, COMMAND. ETA TO THE LZ, TWO MINUTES.
"THIS IS SO COOL."
"IS THIS YOUR FIRST FLIGHT IN A MOLLYMOBILE? I THOUGHT YOU WERE ALREADY RATED AND CLEARED?"

DON'T YOU FRET, DARLIN', THIS ISN'T MY DOLLAR RIDE.*

GOOD, WE HAVE TO STOP SCOTT BEFORE HE CAUSES TOO MUCH DAMAGE.

*FIRST TIME IN A COCKPIT

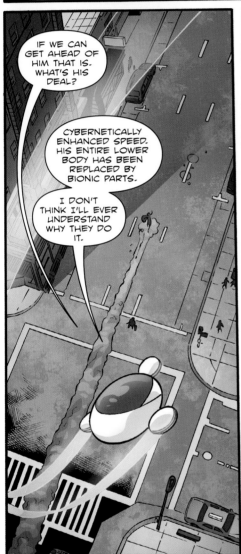

IF WE CAN GET AHEAD OF HIM THAT IS. WHAT'S HIS DEAL?

CYBERNETICALLY ENHANCED SPEED. HIS ENTIRE LOWER BODY HAS BEEN REPLACED BY BIONIC PARTS.

I DON'T THINK I'LL EVER UNDERSTAND WHY THEY DO IT.

WHY WHO DOES WHAT NOW?

SLIPSCOTT, MEDULA, THE OTHERS.

ALTERING THEIR BODIES FOR WHAT, POWER?

DOES IT MATTER? PEOPLE DO BAD THINGS ALL THE TIME.

IT MATTERS TO ME. MAYBE IF I UNDERSTOOD THEM BETTER, I COULD HELP THEM.

YOU REALLY DO CARE, DON'T YOU?

EVERYBODY HAS PAIN THEY DEAL WITH.

UNDERSTANDING THEIR PAIN MAKES IT EASIER TO UNDERSTAND THEM.

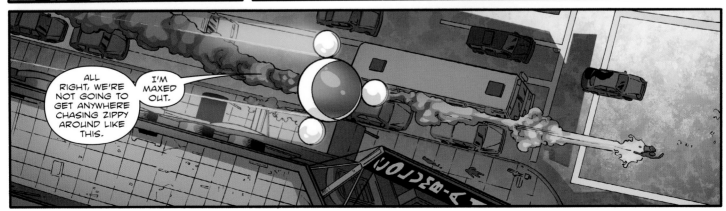

ALL RIGHT, WE'RE NOT GOING TO GET ANYWHERE CHASING ZIPPY AROUND LIKE THIS.

I'M MAXED OUT.

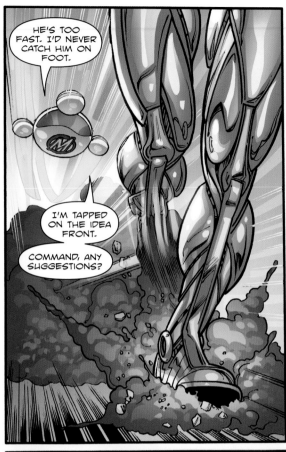

HE'S TOO FAST. I'D NEVER CATCH HIM ON FOOT.

I'M TAPPED ON THE IDEA FRONT.

COMMAND, ANY SUGGESTIONS?

WE'RE SCANNING, PACKAGE. STAND BY.

PACKAGE, WE HAVE MULTIPLE OBSTRUCTIONS ON YOUR 20.

WE'RE FLYING AT ABOUT 40 MILES PER HOUR...

PILOT, STICK TO HIM. I HAVE AN IDEA.

"HOLD HER STEADY AND DO EXACTLY WHAT I SAY."

"GOT YA."

"PACKAGE WHAT ARE YOU DOING?"

STEADY... STEADY...

MOLLY? MOLLY!!

MOLLY! GET BACK IN THAT COCKPIT RIGHT NOW!

NOW! HIT THE BRAKES!

HOOOOAAHHH!

OOF!

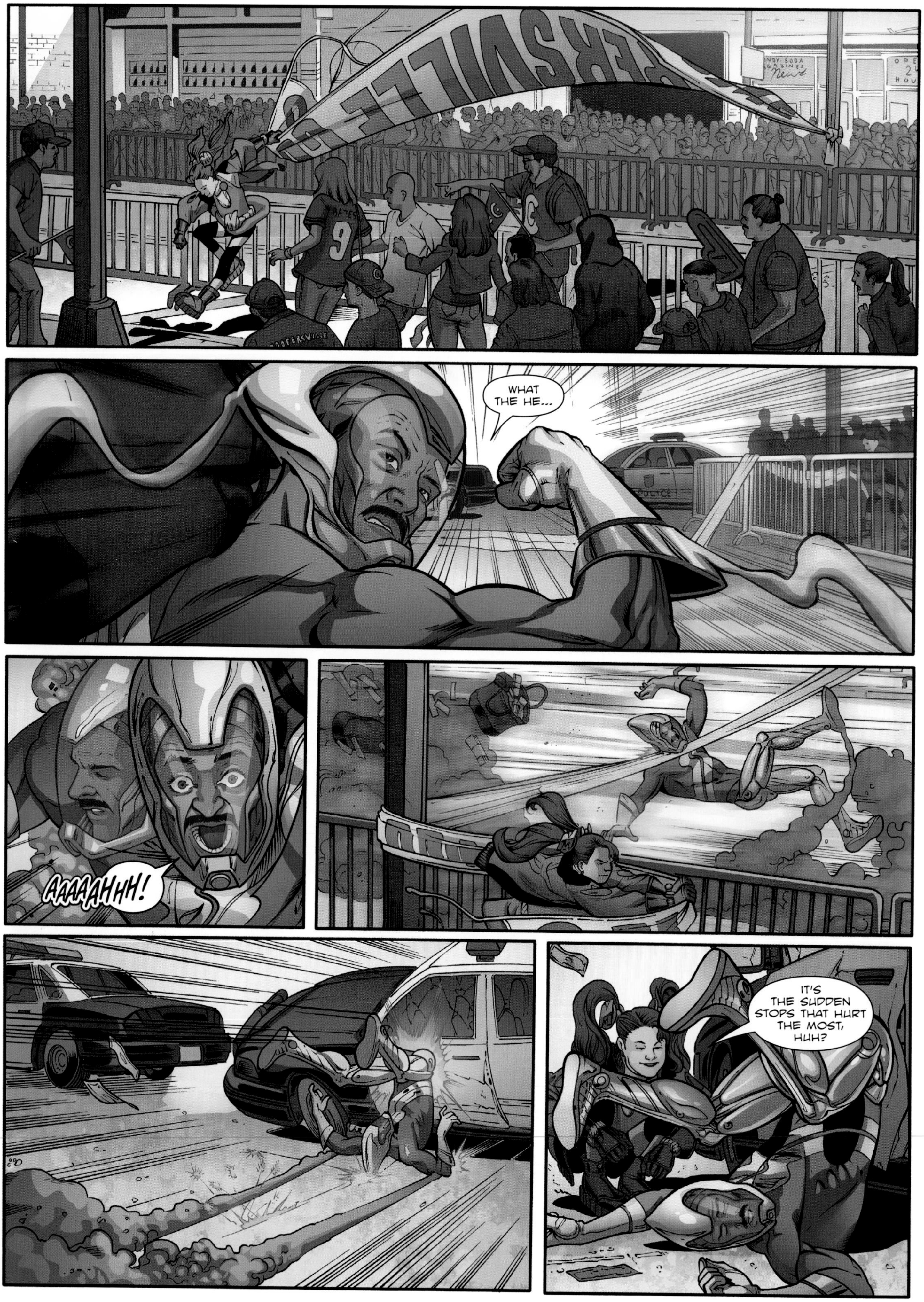
WHAT THE HE...
AAAAAHHH!
IT'S THE SUDDEN STOPS THAT HURT THE MOST, HUH?

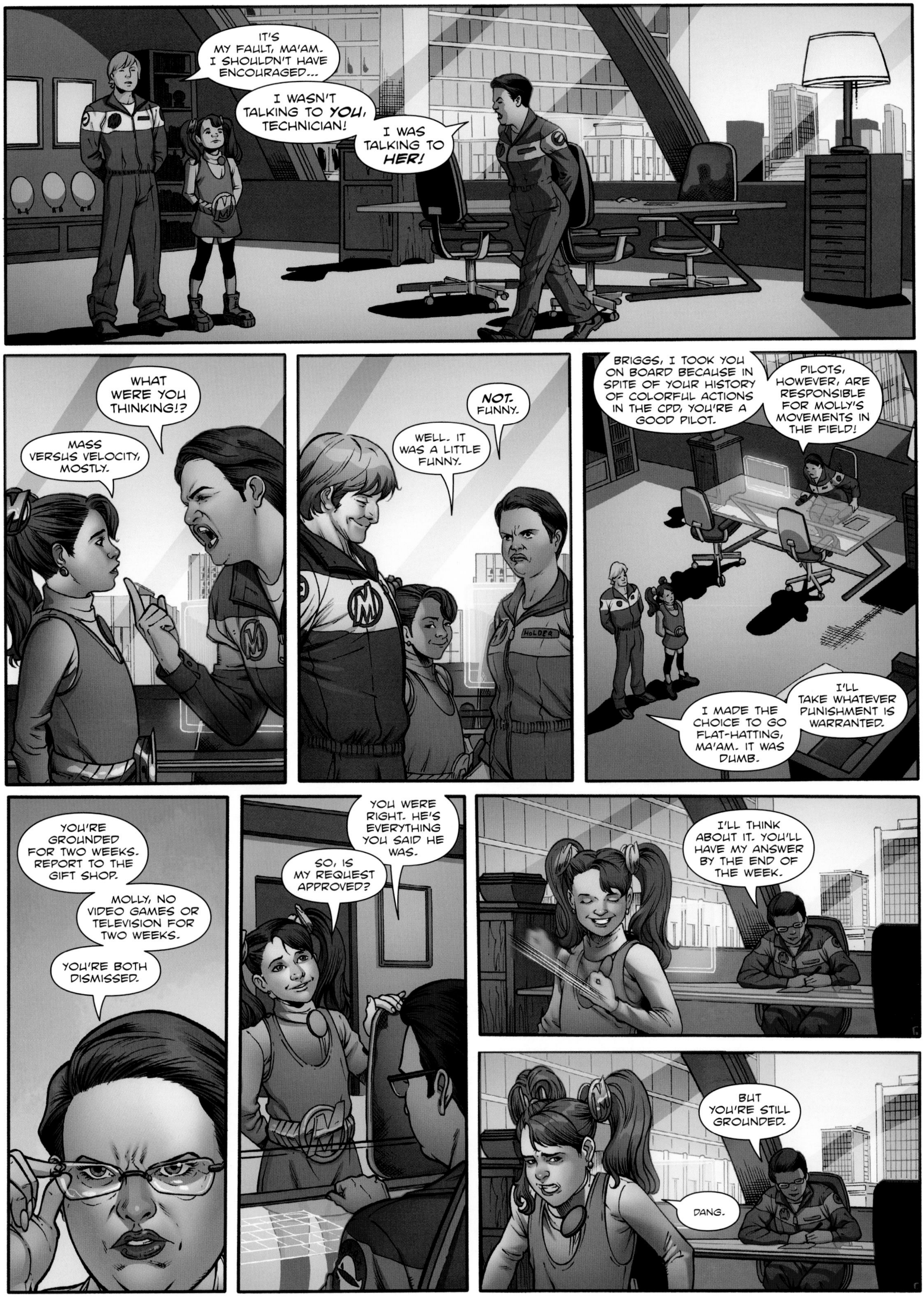

IT'S MY FAULT, MA'AM. I SHOULDN'T HAVE ENCOURAGED...
I WASN'T TALKING TO YOU, TECHNICIAN!
I WAS TALKING TO HER!
WHAT WERE YOU THINKING!?
MASS VERSUS VELOCITY, MOSTLY.
WELL. IT WAS A LITTLE FUNNY.
NOT. FUNNY.
HOLDER
BRIGGS, I TOOK YOU ON BOARD BECAUSE IN SPITE OF YOUR HISTORY OF COLORFUL ACTIONS IN THE CPD, YOU'RE A GOOD PILOT.
PILOTS, HOWEVER, ARE RESPONSIBLE FOR MOLLY'S MOVEMENTS IN THE FIELD!
I'LL TAKE WHATEVER PUNISHMENT IS WARRANTED.
I MADE THE CHOICE TO GO FLAT-HATTING, MA'AM. IT WAS DUMB.
YOU'RE GROUNDED FOR TWO WEEKS. REPORT TO THE GIFT SHOP.
MOLLY, NO VIDEO GAMES OR TELEVISION FOR TWO WEEKS.
YOU'RE BOTH DISMISSED.
YOU WERE RIGHT. HE'S EVERYTHING YOU SAID HE WAS.
SO, IS MY REQUEST APPROVED?
I'LL THINK ABOUT IT. YOU'LL HAVE MY ANSWER BY THE END OF THE WEEK.
BUT YOU'RE STILL GROUNDED.
DANG.

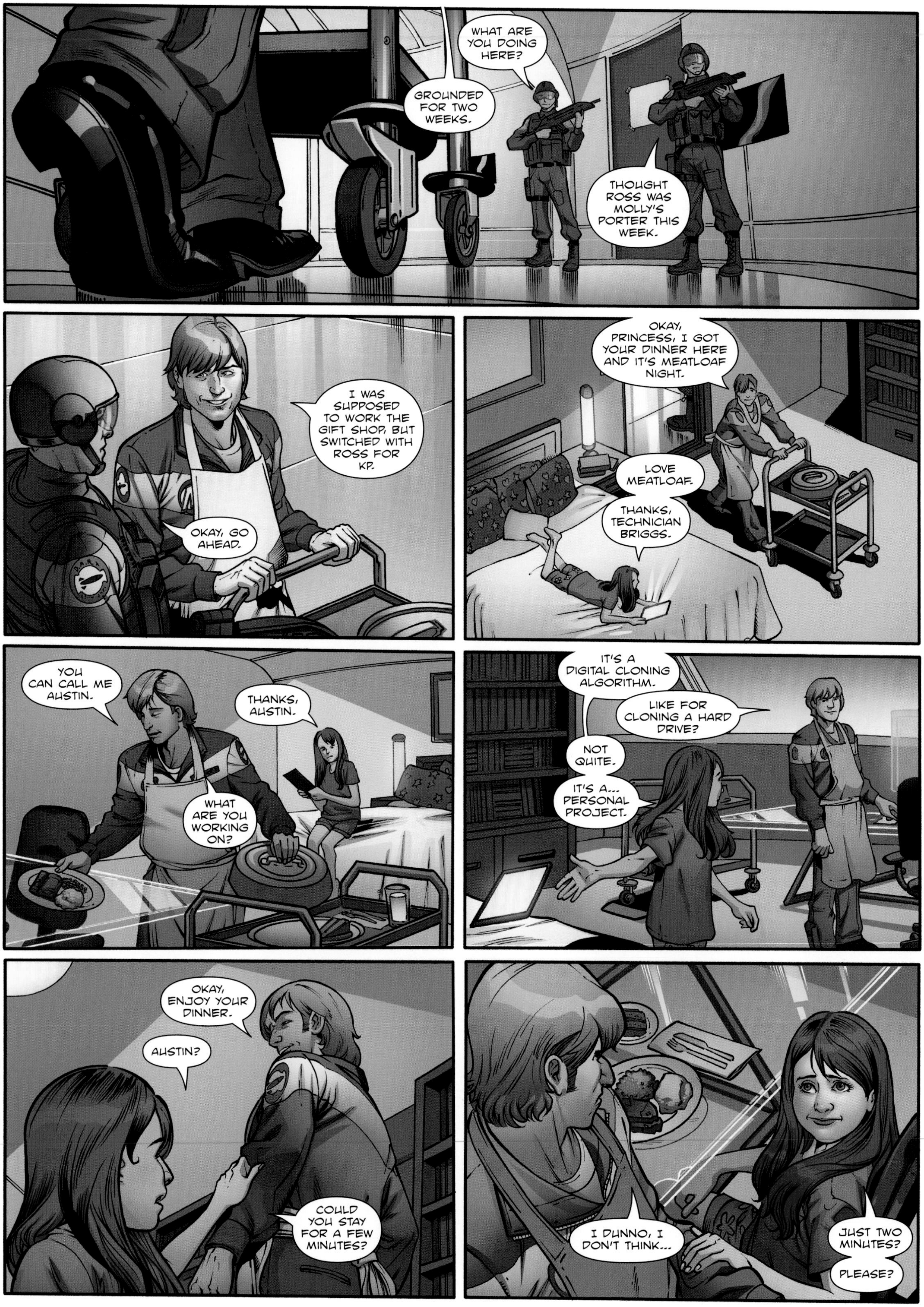

WHAT ARE YOU DOING HERE?
GROUNDED FOR TWO WEEKS.
THOUGHT ROSS WAS MOLLY'S PORTER THIS WEEK.
I WAS SUPPOSED TO WORK THE GIFT SHOP, BUT SWITCHED WITH ROSS FOR KP.
OKAY, GO AHEAD.
OKAY, PRINCESS, I GOT YOUR DINNER HERE AND IT'S MEATLOAF NIGHT.
LOVE MEATLOAF.
THANKS, TECHNICIAN BRIGGS.
YOU CAN CALL ME AUSTIN.
THANKS, AUSTIN.
WHAT ARE YOU WORKING ON?
IT'S A DIGITAL CLONING ALGORITHM.
LIKE FOR CLONING A HARD DRIVE?
NOT QUITE.
IT'S A... PERSONAL PROJECT.
OKAY, ENJOY YOUR DINNER.
AUSTIN?
COULD YOU STAY FOR A FEW MINUTES?
I DUNNO, I DON'T THINK...
JUST TWO MINUTES?
PLEASE?

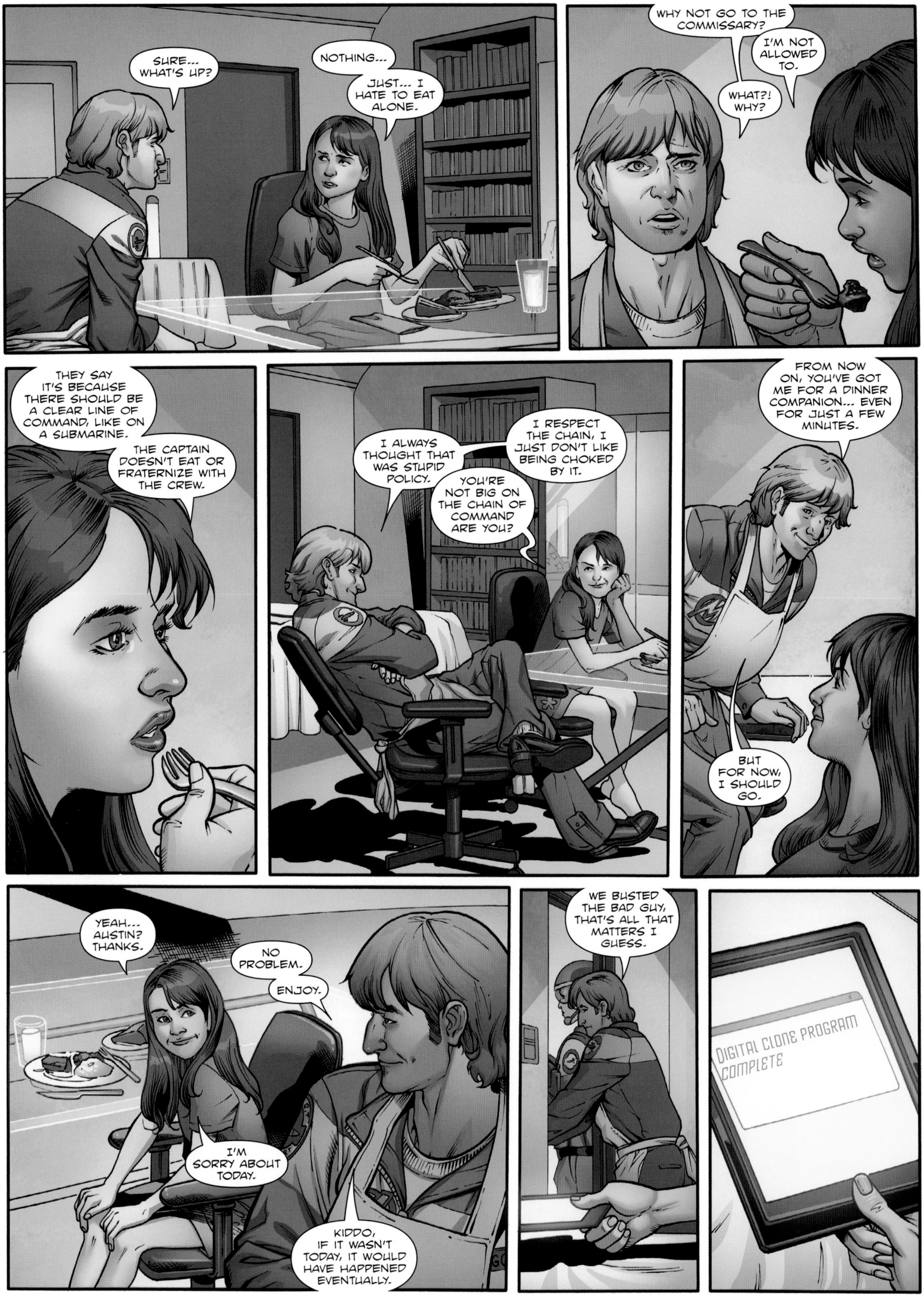
SURE... WHAT'S UP?
NOTHING...
JUST... I HATE TO EAT ALONE.
WHY NOT GO TO THE COMMISSARY?
I'M NOT ALLOWED TO.
WHAT?! WHY?
THEY SAY IT'S BECAUSE THERE SHOULD BE A CLEAR LINE OF COMMAND, LIKE ON A SUBMARINE.
THE CAPTAIN DOESN'T EAT OR FRATERNIZE WITH THE CREW.
I ALWAYS THOUGHT THAT WAS STUPID POLICY.
YOU'RE NOT BIG ON THE CHAIN OF COMMAND ARE YOU?
I RESPECT THE CHAIN, I JUST DON'T LIKE BEING CHOKED BY IT.
FROM NOW ON, YOU'VE GOT ME FOR A DINNER COMPANION... EVEN FOR JUST A FEW MINUTES.
BUT FOR NOW, I SHOULD GO.
YEAH... AUSTIN? THANKS.
NO PROBLEM.
ENJOY.
I'M SORRY ABOUT TODAY.
KIDDO, IF IT WASN'T TODAY, IT WOULD HAVE HAPPENED EVENTUALLY.
WE BUSTED THE BAD GUY, THAT'S ALL THAT MATTERS I GUESS.
DIGITAL CLONE PROGRAM COMPLETE

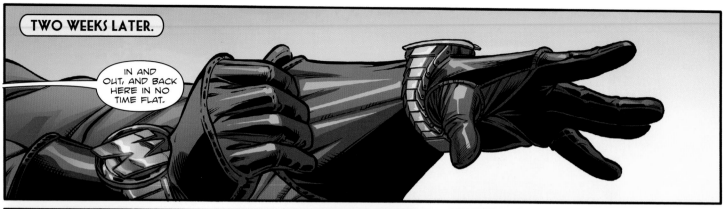

TWO WEEKS LATER.

IN AND OUT, AND BACK HERE IN NO TIME FLAT.

WHAT'S THE SITUATION?

I DON'T KNOW. ALL I WAS TOLD WAS THERE WAS A SUSPICIOUS DISTURBANCE.

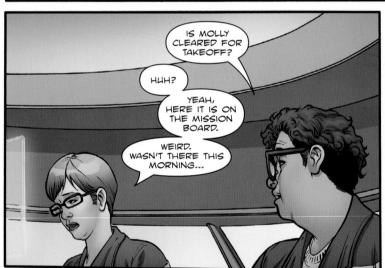

IS MOLLY CLEARED FOR TAKEOFF?

HUH?

YEAH, HERE IT IS ON THE MISSION BOARD.

WEIRD. WASN'T THERE THIS MORNING...

THIS IS WEIRD...

ARE YOU SURE THIS IS THE RIGHT PLACE?

THESE ARE THE COORDINATES IN THE NAV COMPUTER.

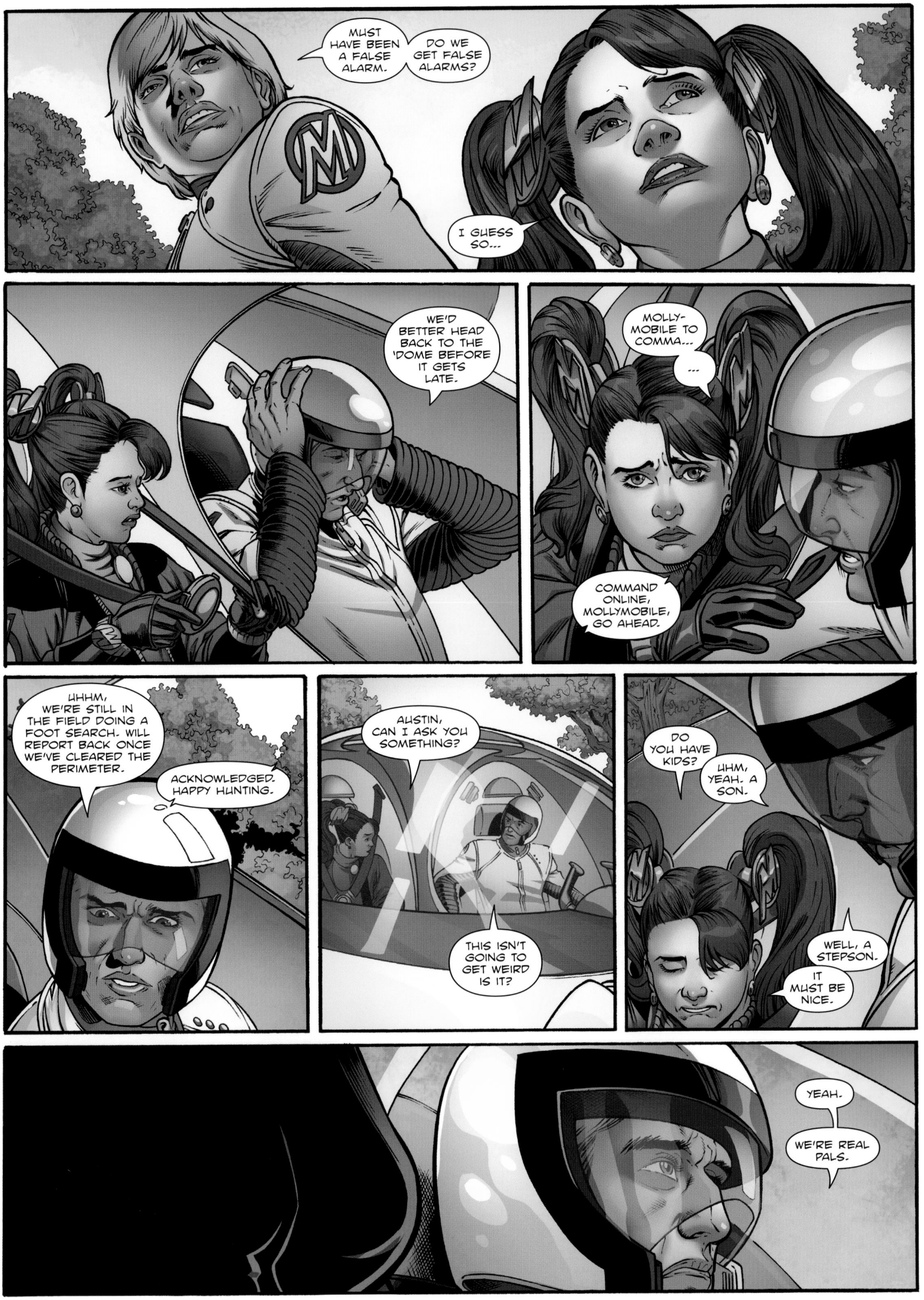
MUST HAVE BEEN A FALSE ALARM.
DO WE GET FALSE ALARMS?
I GUESS SO...
WE'D BETTER HEAD BACK TO THE 'DOME BEFORE IT GETS LATE.
MOLLY-MOBILE TO COMMA...
...
COMMAND ONLINE, MOLLYMOBILE, GO AHEAD.
UHHM, WE'RE STILL IN THE FIELD DOING A FOOT SEARCH. WILL REPORT BACK ONCE WE'VE CLEARED THE PERIMETER.
ACKNOWLEDGED. HAPPY HUNTING.
AUSTIN, CAN I ASK YOU SOMETHING?
THIS ISN'T GOING TO GET WEIRD IS IT?
DO YOU HAVE KIDS?
UHM, YEAH. A SON.
WELL, A STEPSON.
IT MUST BE NICE.
YEAH.
WE'RE REAL PALS.

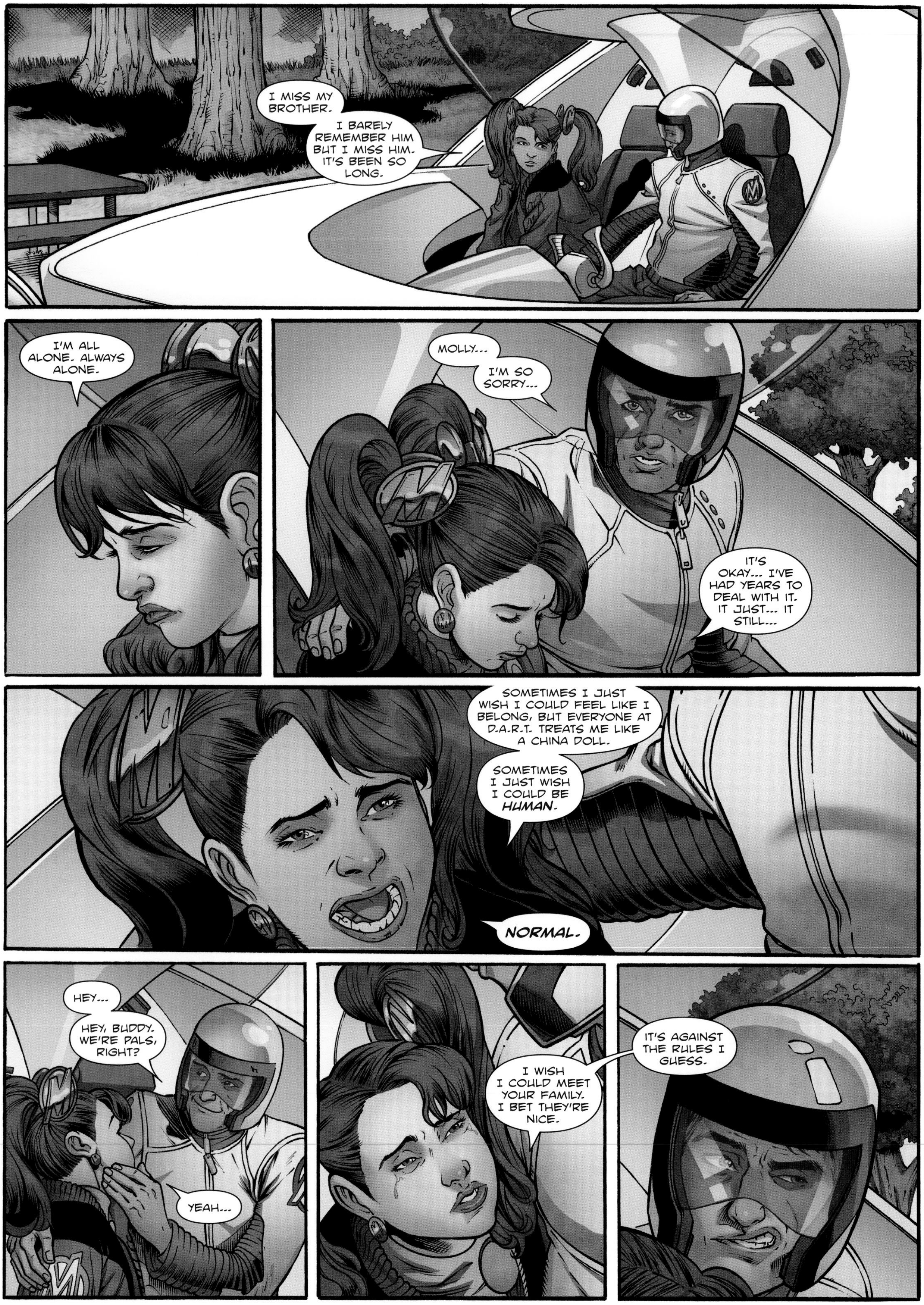
I MISS MY BROTHER.
I BARELY REMEMBER HIM BUT I MISS HIM. IT'S BEEN SO LONG.
I'M ALL ALONE. ALWAYS ALONE.
MOLLY...
I'M SO SORRY...
IT'S OKAY... I'VE HAD YEARS TO DEAL WITH IT. IT JUST... IT STILL...
SOMETIMES I JUST WISH I COULD FEEL LIKE I BELONG, BUT EVERYONE AT D.A.R.T. TREATS ME LIKE A CHINA DOLL.
SOMETIMES I JUST WISH I COULD BE HUMAN.
NORMAL.
HEY...
HEY, BUDDY. WE'RE PALS, RIGHT?
YEAH...
I WISH I COULD MEET YOUR FAMILY. I BET THEY'RE NICE.
IT'S AGAINST THE RULES I GUESS.

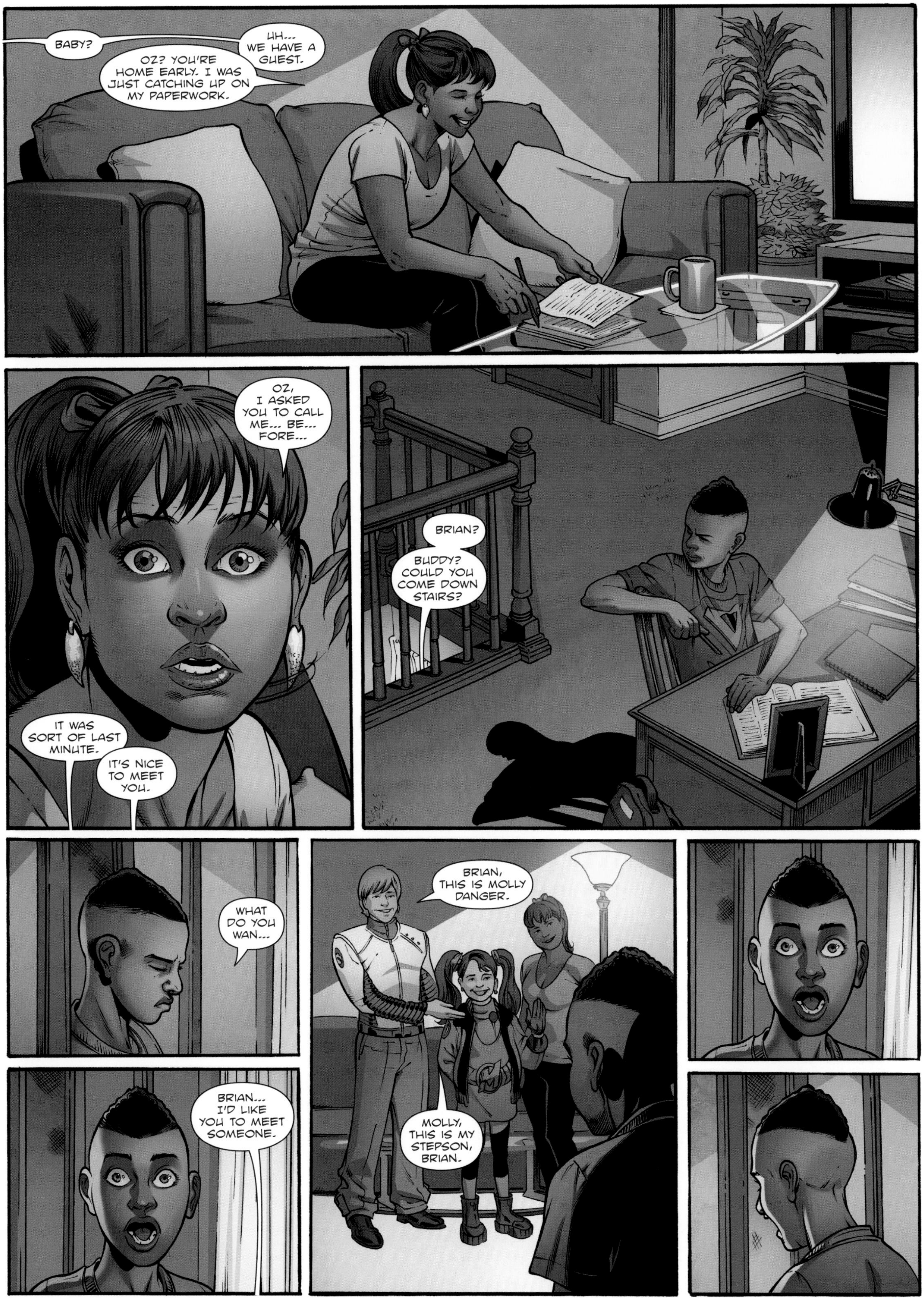
BABY?
OZ? YOU'RE HOME EARLY. I WAS JUST CATCHING UP ON MY PAPERWORK.
UH... WE HAVE A GUEST.
OZ, I ASKED YOU TO CALL ME... BE... FORE...
IT WAS SORT OF LAST MINUTE.
IT'S NICE TO MEET YOU.
BRIAN?
BUDDY? COULD YOU COME DOWN STAIRS?
WHAT DO YOU WAN...
BRIAN... I'D LIKE YOU TO MEET SOMEONE.
BRIAN, THIS IS MOLLY DANGER.
MOLLY, THIS IS MY STEPSON, BRIAN.

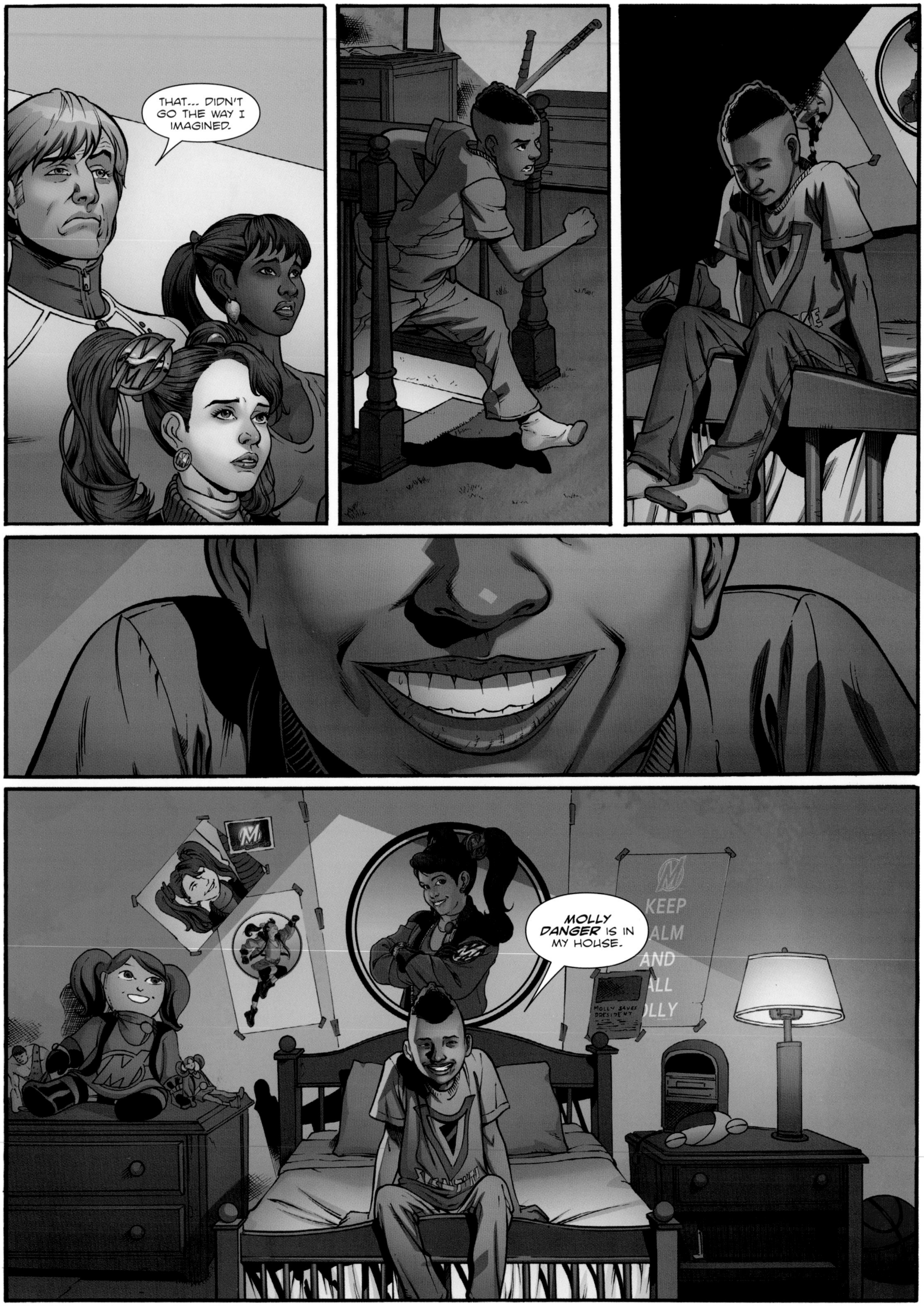
THAT... DIDN'T GO THE WAY I IMAGINED.
KEEP
ALM
AND
ALL
OLLY
MOLLY SAVES PRESIDENT
MOLLY DANGER IS IN MY HOUSE.

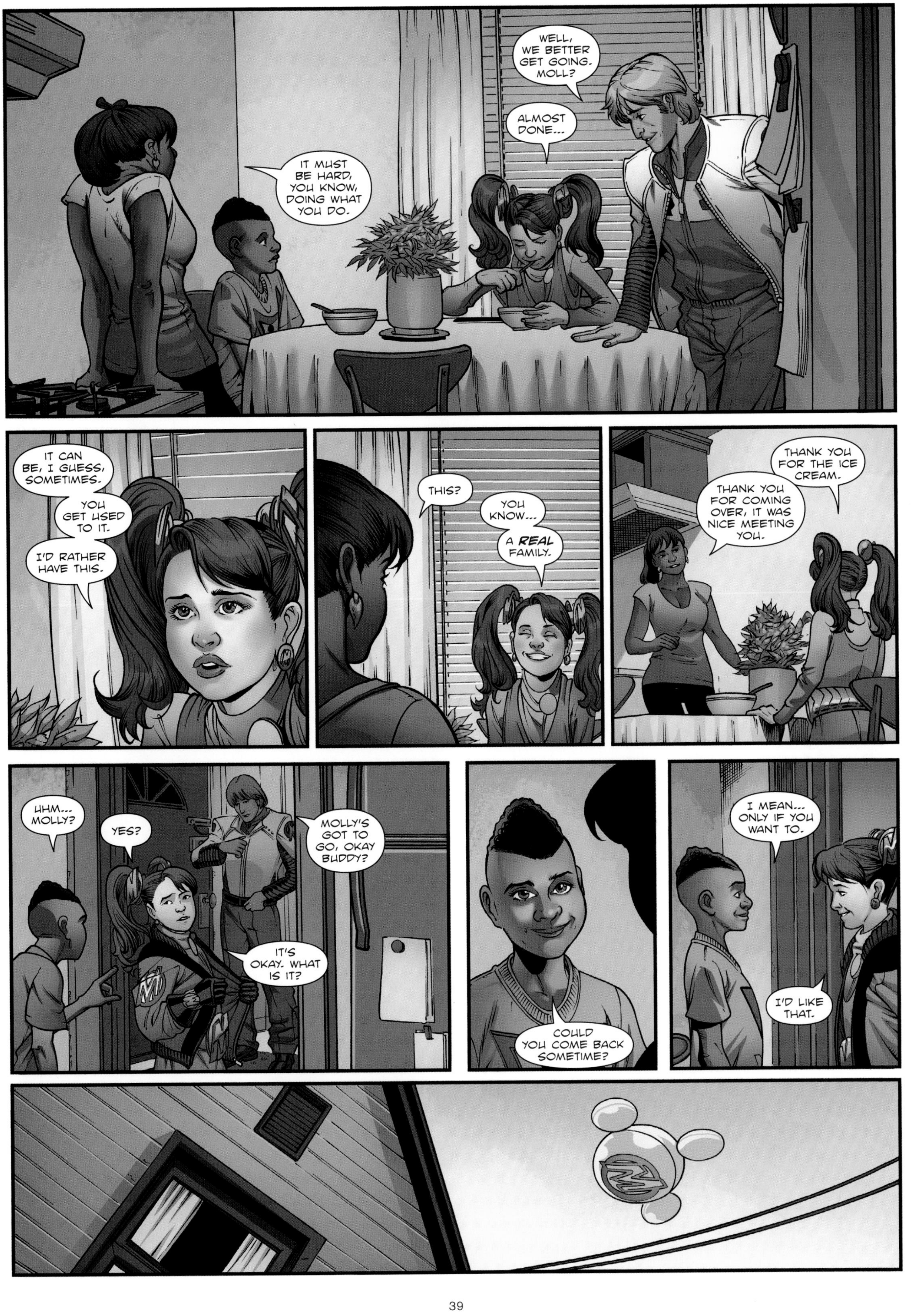

WELL, WE BETTER GET GOING. MOLL?
ALMOST DONE...
IT MUST BE HARD, YOU KNOW, DOING WHAT YOU DO.
IT CAN BE, I GUESS, SOMETIMES.
YOU GET USED TO IT.
I'D RATHER HAVE THIS.
THIS?
YOU KNOW...
A **REAL** FAMILY.
THANK YOU FOR THE ICE CREAM.
THANK YOU FOR COMING OVER, IT WAS NICE MEETING YOU.
UHM... MOLLY?
YES?
MOLLY'S GOT TO GO, OKAY BUDDY?
IT'S OKAY. WHAT IS IT?
COULD YOU COME BACK SOMETIME?
I MEAN... ONLY IF YOU WANT TO.
I'D LIKE THAT.

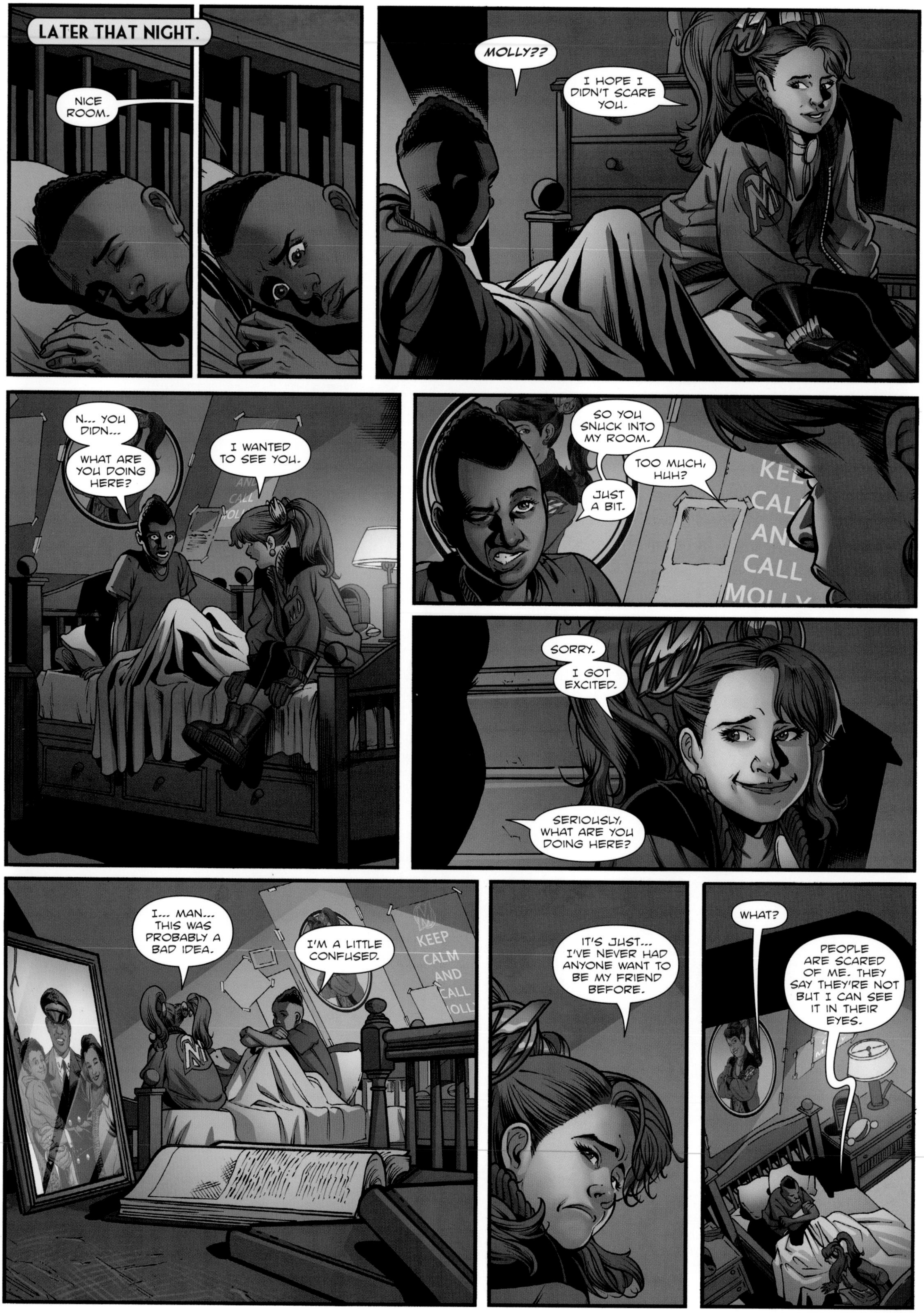

LATER THAT NIGHT.
NICE ROOM.
MOLLY??
I HOPE I DIDN'T SCARE YOU.
N... YOU DIDN...
WHAT ARE YOU DOING HERE?
I WANTED TO SEE YOU.
SO YOU SNUCK INTO MY ROOM.
TOO MUCH, HUH?
JUST A BIT.
KEEP CALM AND CALL MOLLY
SORRY. I GOT EXCITED.
SERIOUSLY, WHAT ARE YOU DOING HERE?
I... MAN... THIS WAS PROBABLY A BAD IDEA.
I'M A LITTLE CONFUSED.
KEEP CALM AND CALL
IT'S JUST... I'VE NEVER HAD ANYONE WANT TO BE MY FRIEND BEFORE.
WHAT?
PEOPLE ARE SCARED OF ME. THEY SAY THEY'RE NOT BUT I CAN SEE IT IN THEIR EYES.

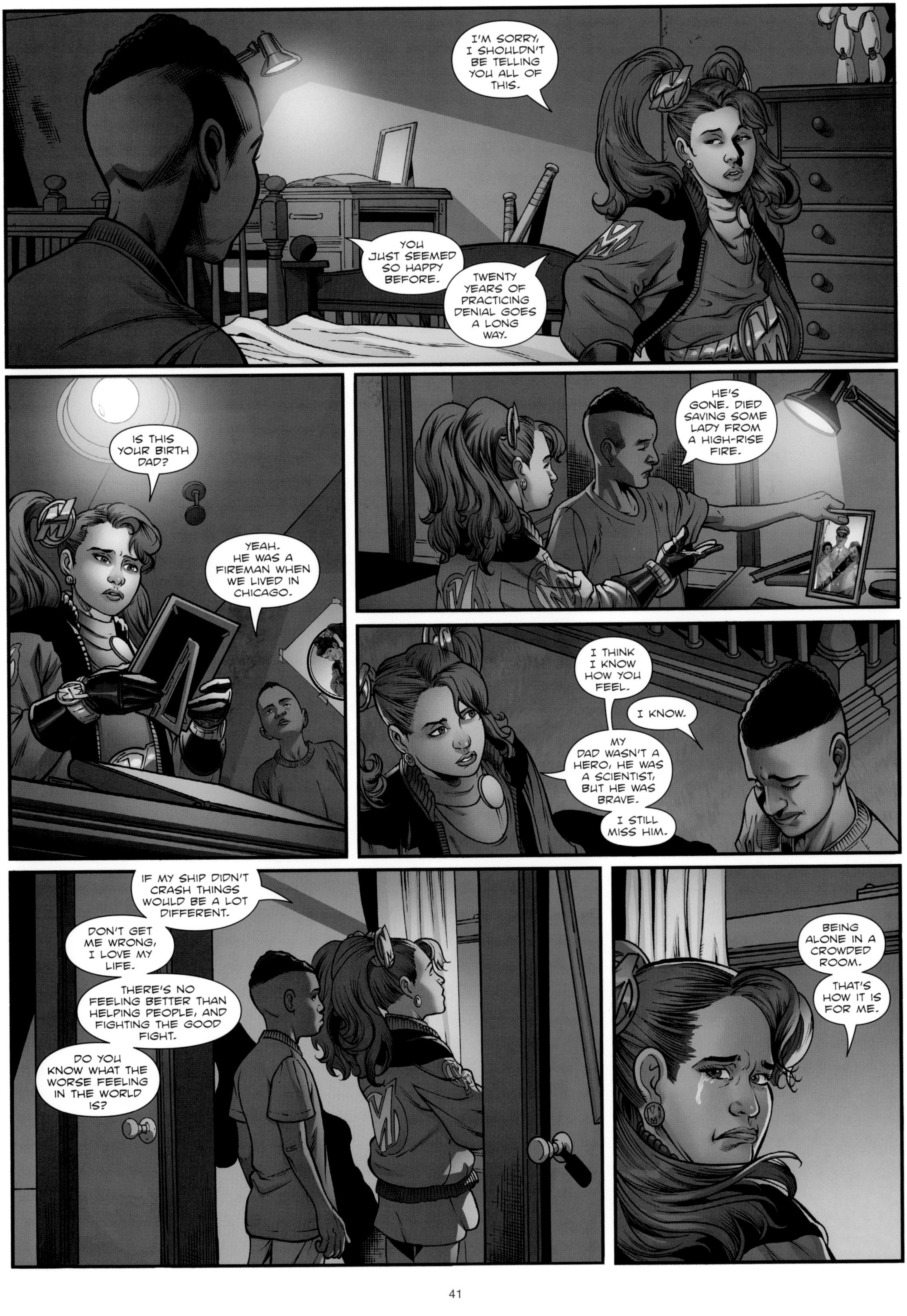
I'M SORRY, I SHOULDN'T BE TELLING YOU ALL OF THIS.
YOU JUST SEEMED SO HAPPY BEFORE.
TWENTY YEARS OF PRACTICING DENIAL GOES A LONG WAY.
IS THIS YOUR BIRTH DAD?
YEAH. HE WAS A FIREMAN WHEN WE LIVED IN CHICAGO.
HE'S GONE. DIED SAVING SOME LADY FROM A HIGH-RISE FIRE.
I THINK I KNOW HOW YOU FEEL.
I KNOW.
MY DAD WASN'T A HERO, HE WAS A SCIENTIST, BUT HE WAS BRAVE.
I STILL MISS HIM.
IF MY SHIP DIDN'T CRASH THINGS WOULD BE A LOT DIFFERENT.
DON'T GET ME WRONG, I LOVE MY LIFE.
THERE'S NO FEELING BETTER THAN HELPING PEOPLE, AND FIGHTING THE GOOD FIGHT.
DO YOU KNOW WHAT THE WORSE FEELING IN THE WORLD IS?
BEING ALONE IN A CROWDED ROOM.
THAT'S HOW IT IS FOR ME.

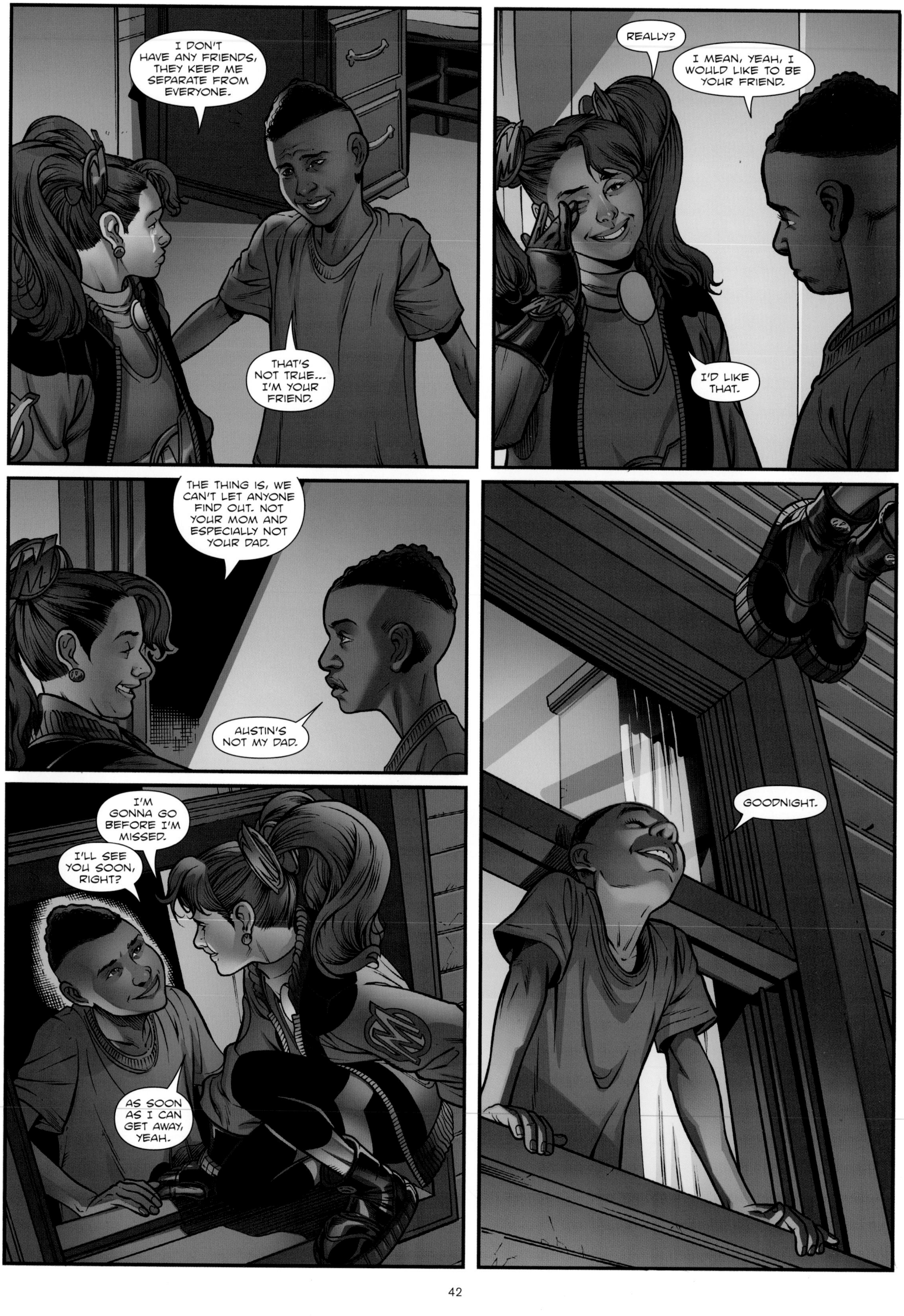
I DON'T HAVE ANY FRIENDS, THEY KEEP ME SEPARATE FROM EVERYONE.
THAT'S NOT TRUE... I'M YOUR FRIEND.
REALLY?
I MEAN, YEAH, I WOULD LIKE TO BE YOUR FRIEND.
I'D LIKE THAT.
THE THING IS, WE CAN'T LET ANYONE FIND OUT. NOT YOUR MOM AND ESPECIALLY NOT YOUR DAD.
AUSTIN'S NOT MY DAD.
I'M GONNA GO BEFORE I'M MISSED.
I'LL SEE YOU SOON, RIGHT?
AS SOON AS I CAN GET AWAY, YEAH.
GOODNIGHT.

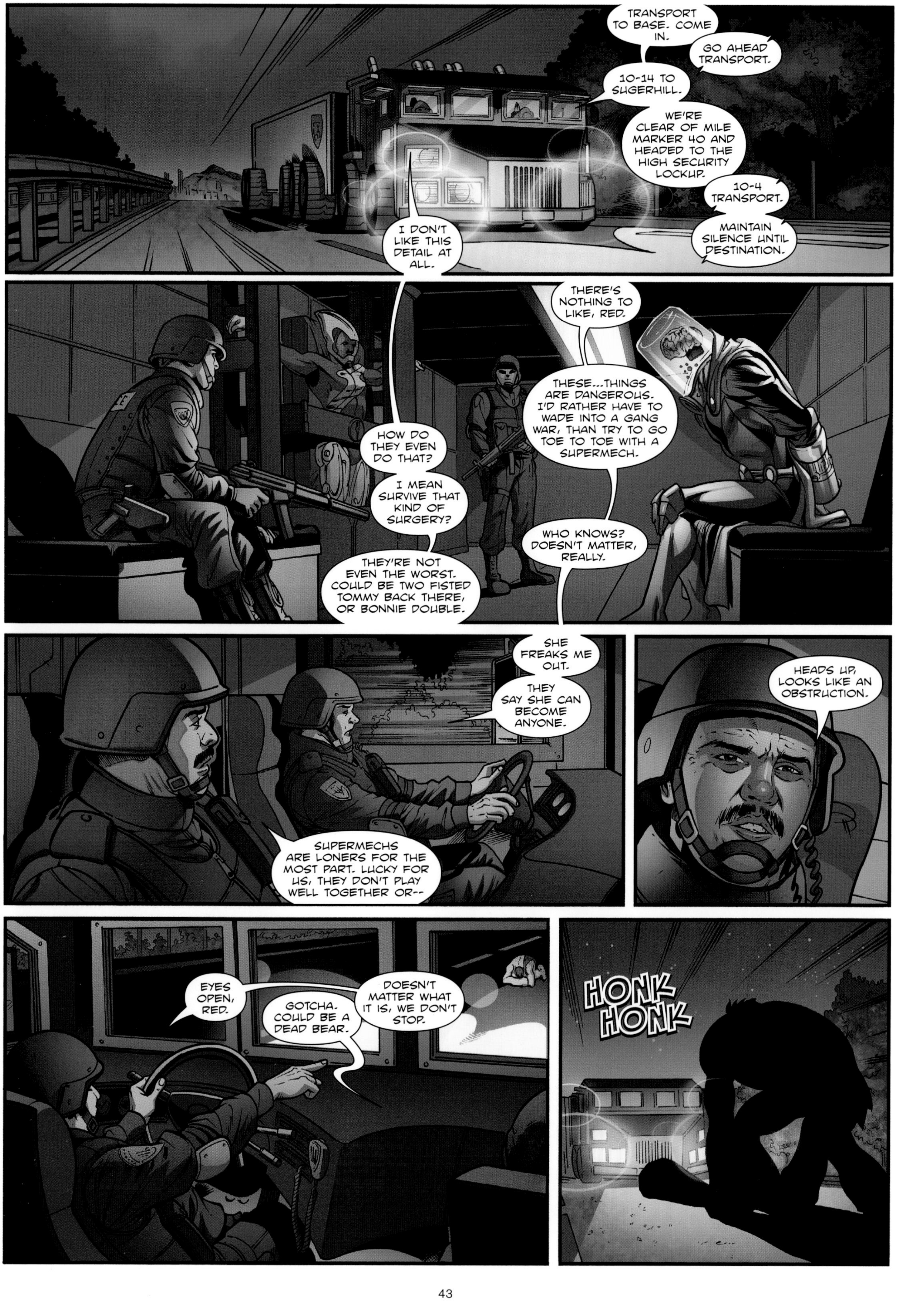
TRANSPORT TO BASE. COME IN.
GO AHEAD TRANSPORT.
10-14 TO SUGERHILL.
WE'RE CLEAR OF MILE MARKER 40 AND HEADED TO THE HIGH SECURITY LOCKUP.
10-4 TRANSPORT.
MAINTAIN SILENCE UNTIL DESTINATION.
I DON'T LIKE THIS DETAIL AT ALL.
THERE'S NOTHING TO LIKE, RED.
THESE...THINGS ARE DANGEROUS. I'D RATHER HAVE TO WADE INTO A GANG WAR, THAN TRY TO GO TOE TO TOE WITH A SUPERMECH.
HOW DO THEY EVEN DO THAT?
I MEAN SURVIVE THAT KIND OF SURGERY?
WHO KNOWS? DOESN'T MATTER, REALLY.
THEY'RE NOT EVEN THE WORST. COULD BE TWO FISTED TOMMY BACK THERE, OR BONNIE DOUBLE.
SHE FREAKS ME OUT.
THEY SAY SHE CAN BECOME ANYONE.
SUPERMECHS ARE LONERS FOR THE MOST PART. LUCKY FOR US, THEY DON'T PLAY WELL TOGETHER OR--
HEADS UP, LOOKS LIKE AN OBSTRUCTION.
EYES OPEN, RED.
GOTCHA. COULD BE A DEAD BEAR.
DOESN'T MATTER WHAT IT IS, WE DON'T STOP.
HONK HONK

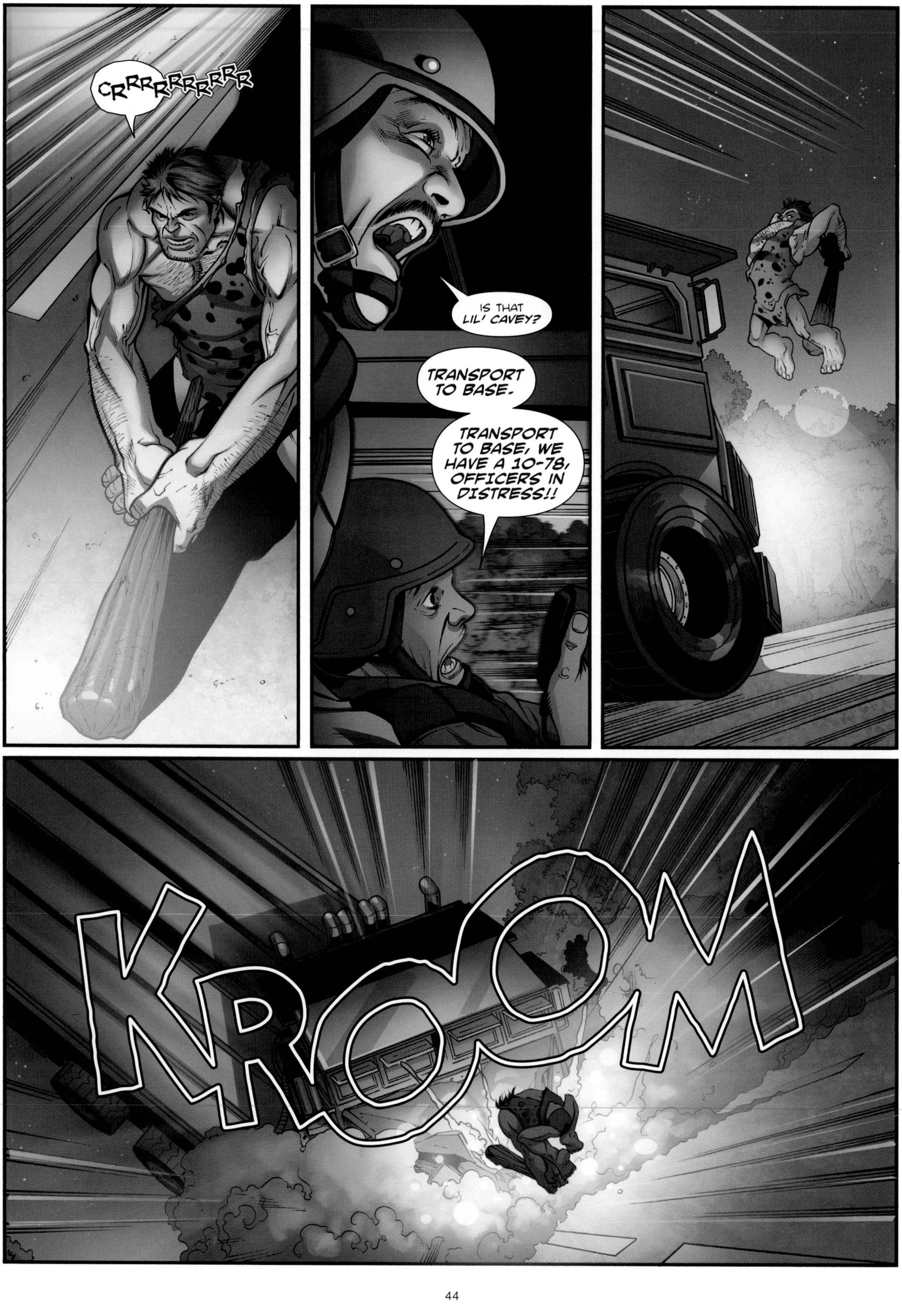
CRRRRRRRRRR
IS THAT LIL' CAVEY?
TRANSPORT TO BASE.
TRANSPORT TO BASE, WE HAVE A 10-78, OFFICERS IN DISTRESS!!
KROOM

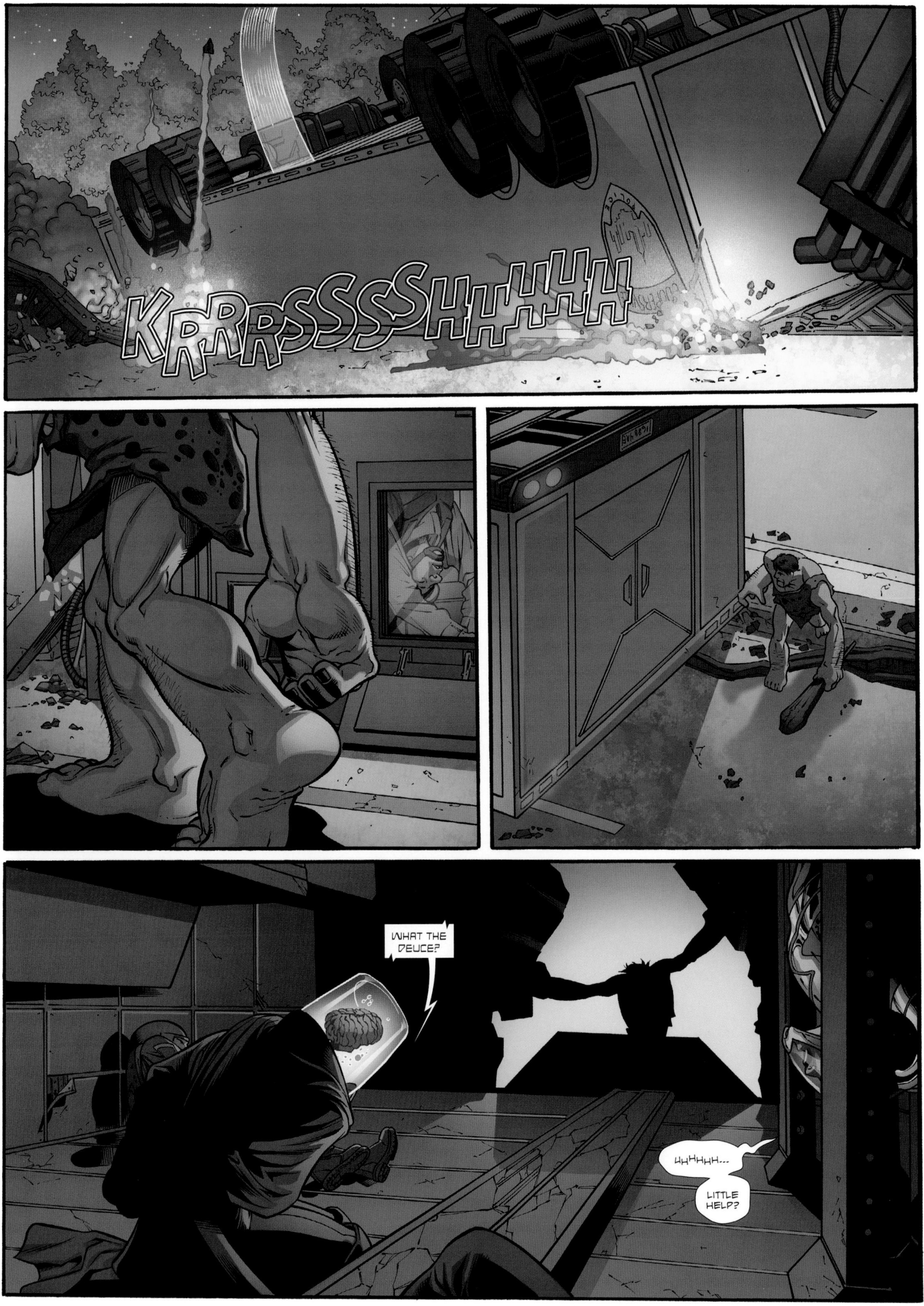
KRRRSSSSHHHHHH
WHAT THE DEUCE?
UHHHHHH...
LITTLE HELP?

FREE.

WELL... THANK YOU... LIL' CAVEY.

I'LL BE ON MY WAY THEN.

NO... CAN'T... GO.

EXCUSE ME?

OOF!

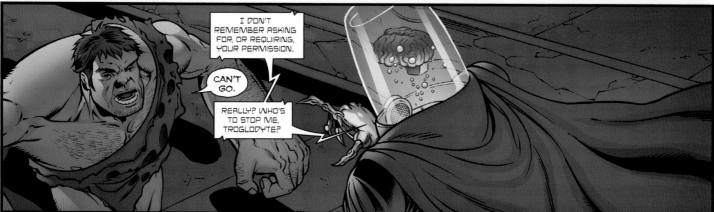

I DON'T REMEMBER ASKING FOR, OR REQUIRING, YOUR PERMISSION.

CAN'T GO.

REALLY? WHO'S TO STOP ME, TROGLODYTE?

FATHER.

NO...

FATHER? WHO THE HELL IS FATHER?

YOUR FATHER.

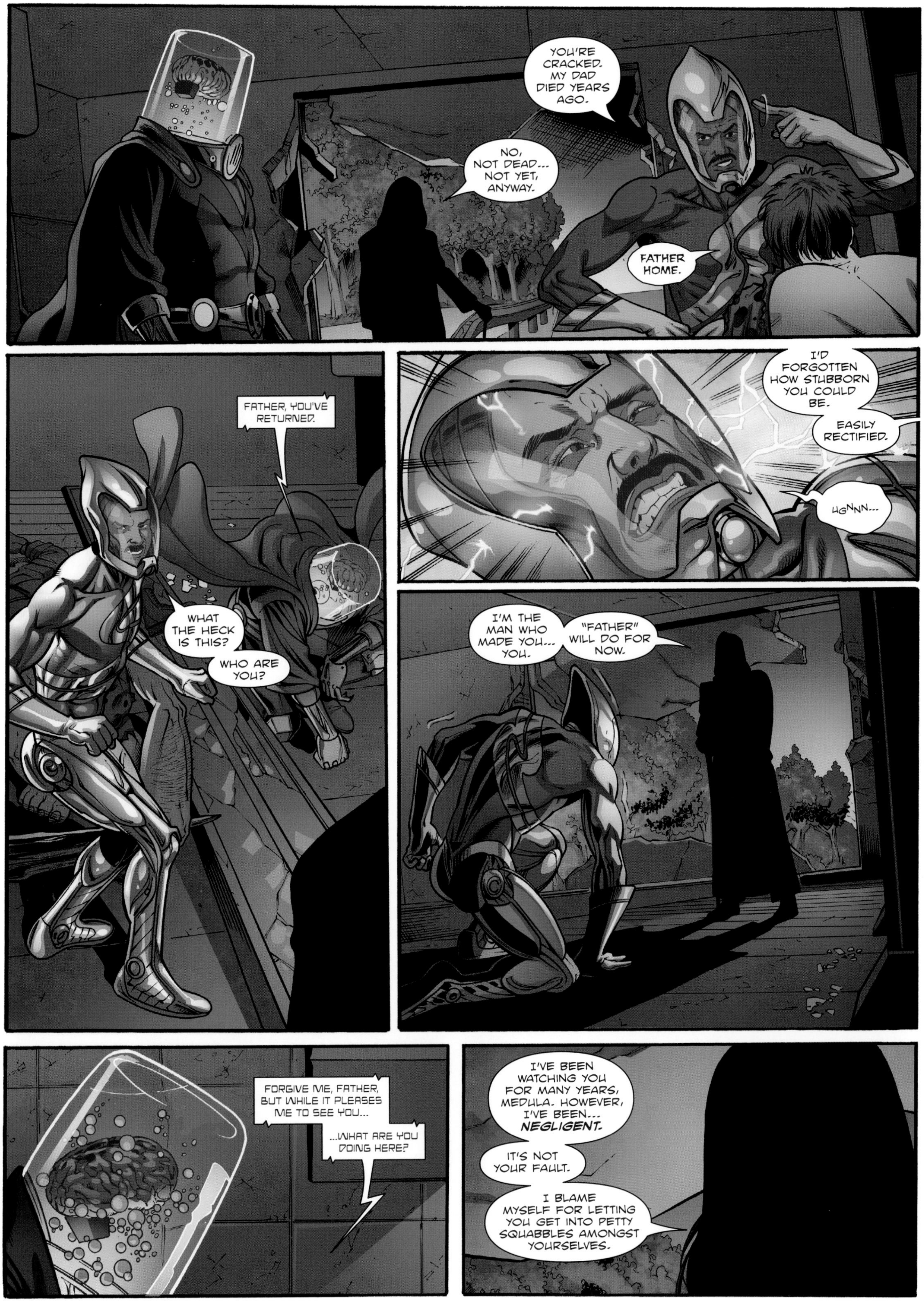

YOU'RE CRACKED. MY DAD DIED YEARS AGO.
NO, NOT DEAD... NOT YET, ANYWAY.
FATHER HOME.
FATHER, YOU'VE RETURNED.
WHAT THE HECK IS THIS?
WHO ARE YOU?
I'D FORGOTTEN HOW STUBBORN YOU COULD BE.
EASILY RECTIFIED.
UGNNN...
I'M THE MAN WHO MADE YOU... YOU.
"FATHER" WILL DO FOR NOW.
FORGIVE ME, FATHER, BUT WHILE IT PLEASES ME TO SEE YOU...
...WHAT ARE YOU DOING HERE?
I'VE BEEN WATCHING YOU FOR MANY YEARS, MEDULA. HOWEVER, I'VE BEEN... NEGLIGENT.
IT'S NOT YOUR FAULT.
I BLAME MYSELF FOR LETTING YOU GET INTO PETTY SQUABBLES AMONGST YOURSELVES.

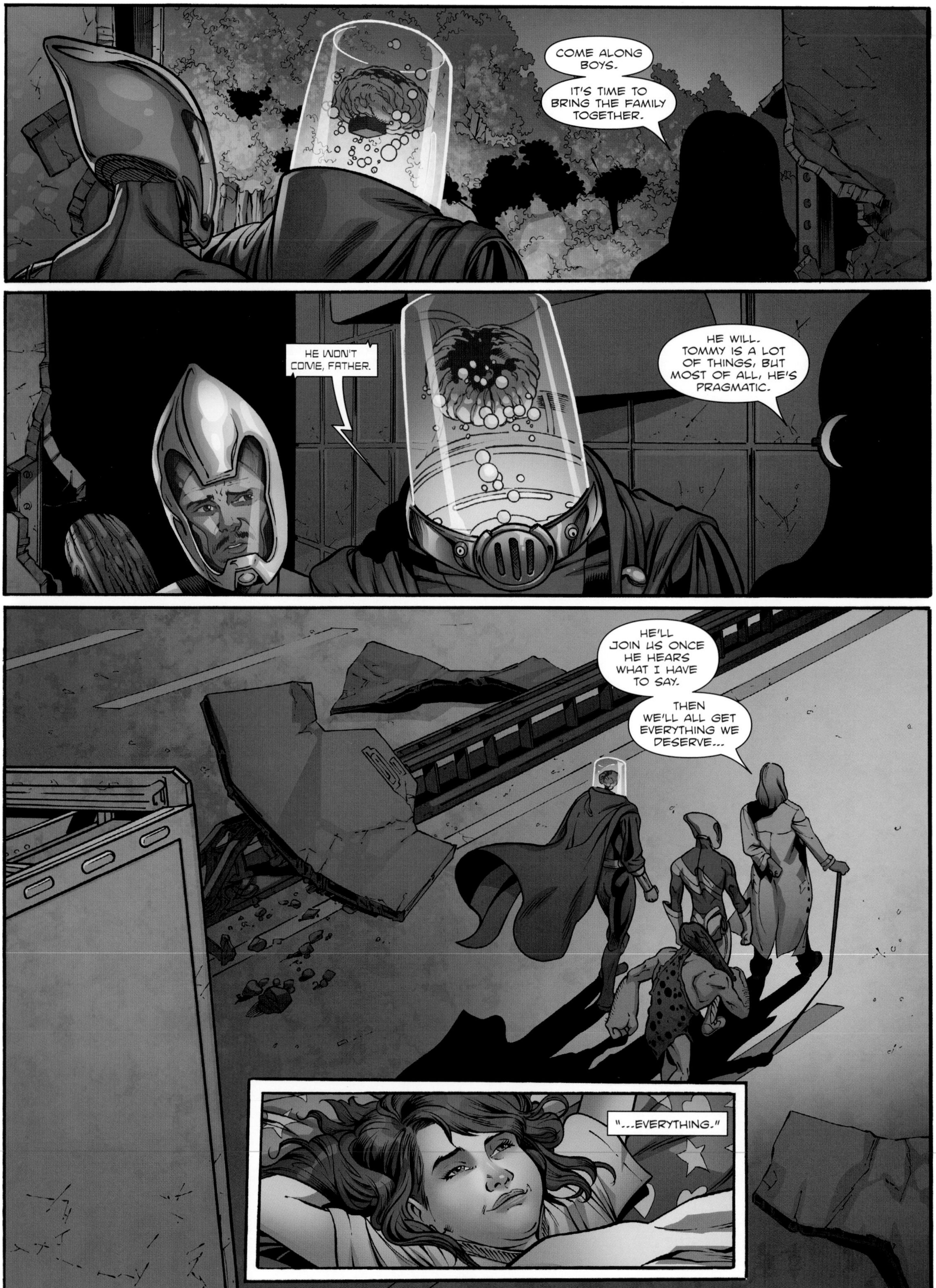
COME ALONG BOYS.
IT'S TIME TO BRING THE FAMILY TOGETHER.
HE WON'T COME, FATHER.
HE WILL. TOMMY IS A LOT OF THINGS, BUT MOST OF ALL, HE'S PRAGMATIC.
HE'LL JOIN US ONCE HE HEARS WHAT I HAVE TO SAY.
THEN WE'LL ALL GET EVERYTHING WE DESERVE...
"...EVERYTHING."

THIS PROJECT COULD NOT HAVE BEEN COMPLETED WITHOUT THE GENEROSITY OF THE FOLLOWING PEOPLE WITHOUT YOU AND FUNDING PLATFORMS LIKE KICKSTARTER, MOLLY DANGER WOULD NOT HAVE BECOME A REALITY

Michelle Das | Jorge Carlos II Cavazos Galas | Hilary Stewart | Fernando Del Bosque | Eric Sellers | Sam Gavin | David Olbrich | David Zerenga | Dorocq Francoise | Jeff Streeter | Jon Carroll | Lisa Wilber | Robert W. Triplett | Michael Hartmann | Andrew Dynon | David Macho | Albert Lei | Chris Buchner | David Chamberlain | Jim Hardison | Kathleen Hanrahan | Michael Rankins | Nicholas Kives | Shannon Weathers | David Spencer | Jarrod Selsmark | Ethan Zoller | Robert Atkins | Ryan Drost | Wayne Mousseau | Larry Bishop | Natalie Nelson | Anthony Joas | Brandon Eaker | Brian Petkash | Dana Rae | Daniel Govar | Dave Belmore | Dev Madan | Devany Brown | Felix Gallo | Greg Evans | Janelle Asselin | Jason Cany | Jeffrey Moy | Jen Sparenberg | Jeremy Bement | John Colagioia | Joseph D Fobbs | Kathryn Trabert | Keith Ambrose | Keith Williams | Kevin T. Brown | Lauren M. Barrett | Michael Gulick | Tim Meakins | Tony Rivas | William Goodman | Brett Danalake | Lauren Perry | Austyn J. Berry | Carsten Immel | Marisa Pintado | Peter Goulborn | Trevor Boyd | Caanan Grall | Kris Miranda | Ryan Steans | Travis Skinner | Jacques Nyemb | Keith Kahla | Kevin Quass | Kevin Zimmerman | Nicole Cammarata | Sarah Spear | Daniel Reed | Elizabeth Cady | Elsa Guerena | Janel Andersen | Kurt Roggendorf | Michelle Manning | Mike Campbell | Samuel Gaudreau | Richard Mclean | Brian Christman | Kofi Jamal Simmons | Andrew Bennett | Aabra Jaggard | Ahmed Omar Shaban | Alan Sparrow | Alan White | Aldo Palmieri | Alex De Campi | Alexa Tigre | Alexander Lagos | Alexandra Benson | Alexis Carpenter | Allen Nilles | Anthony Spay | Bernadette Walker | Bill Ritter | Bj Dowd | Bob Ingersoll | Brendan Tihane | Brett Schenker | Brett Strassner | Brian Warren | Cameron/Dcbs | Chris Mack | Chris O'hearn | Chris Vincent | Chris Ward | Chuck Childers | Clifford Parmeter | Adam Withers | Craig Rousseau | Cyndie Bradburn | Daanon Decock | Dan Ichimoto | Daphne Talusani | Dave Dwonch | Dirk Dougherty | Don Keeney | Drew Bancroft | Emily Lafond | Erin Hawley | Fred Van Lente | Gail Knowles | Gary Beason | Giacomo Santangelo | Glenn Carrere | Glenn Like | Ian Moore | J.r. Lemar | Janice Cohen/Mike Carlin | Jason G. Michalski | Jason Rinn | Javier Cruz Winnik | Jd Ferries-Rowe | Jd Hancock | Jen Van Meter | Jessica Brown | Jill Pantozzi | Jim McClain | Joe Boudrie | Johan Hernandez | John Ward | Jonathon Paton | Joseph Dowling | Josh Matsuya | Joshua Emmons | Karla Manson | Kaya Casper | Keith Dallas | Ken Mcfarlane | Kendra Mealy Wilk | Kenny Lynch | Kevin Lansford | Kim Pallister | Kristy Quinn | Marc Deering | Mark Geier | Mark Stegbauer | Martha Thomases | Matthew Miller | Maya Keshavan | Melissa Hammon | Michael Hew Wing | Michael Royle | Michele Haggar | Mike Thomas | Mitch Benn | Molly Nece | Monica Rocha | Nancy Corey | Nicole Tucker | Nova Morris | Patrick Tipps | Paula Hidalgo | Pauline Benney | Peter Lange | Rey De Joya | Rhiannon Kaye | Rich Noseworthy | Robert Greenwood | Robert Ruddell | Rosemary Soule | Sally Robinson | Scott Iskow | Scott Pemberton | Scott Rowland | Sean Whelan | Shiny Buttons | Stacy Korn | Stephanie Wooten | Steve Walker | Thomas Brincefield | Thomas Morrill | Tim Spencer | Timothy Dierks | Vinnie | William T Carpenter Jr. | Wyatt Eddy | Adan Tejada | Brent Christian | Victoria Pagac | Catie Murphy | Mohamad Aziz Salim | Nikita Bandaru | Patricia Schlithler Da Fonseca Cardoso | Stuart Moore | Andrew J Moore | Ryan Lavender | Jamian Evans | Andreas Seeger | Andrew Batchelor | Debra Chapman | Leslie Moore | Mathias Rïüyrvik | Megan Argent | Paul Godsil | Rodolfo Orlandi | A-J Mcgarry-Thickitt | Andrew Wilson | Andy Lanning | Baptiste Lepilleur | Benedict Durbin | Bjïürn Reinhart Mertinat Kolstad | Cassandra James | Cormac Dullaghan | Craig Blackwood | David Makin | Davina Gifford | Elin Macbrayne | Fergus Maximus | Frederic Lorge | James Wallis | John Dalton | Julia Brooking-Trypanis | Lukas Adler | Matt Haswell | Michael Holzgruber | Mr William Johnston | Paul Cornell | Renard Bertrand | Richard Morgan | Robert Mcintyre | Sarah Littlehales | Shaun Walsh | Stefan Linden | Calvin Hall | Joseph Illidge | Shane Harsch | Karen Mahoney | Tehani Wessely | Bellan Dye | Bianca Woods | Corwin C Crowl | Eve England-Markun | Faith Shergold | Frank Krulicki | Grant Mclaughlin | Howard Fein | James Hillier | Jason Hall | John Macleod | Jose Antonio Garcia Lopez | Karine Charlebois | Kathleen Ralph | Katrina Lehto | Keith Miller | Kenneth Trainer | Kevin Babineau | Mark Foo | Matt Chaput | Michael Faber | Michael Lucich | Philippe Boulle | Rodney Carter | Stephen Wark | Trenton Broens | Hal Halbert | Aaron Devrick | Aaron Hunter | Aaron Jones | Abigail Fetterman | Adam Coker | Adam Dekraker | Adam J. Monetta | Adam P Knave | Alec Burkhardt | Alex Dueben | Alex Harrison | Alison Brummer | Allen Ashworth | Amanda Mcpeck | Amanda Wetherhold | Andrew J. Hayford | Andrew Kaplan | Andrew Williams | Andy Erickson | Andy Harris | Anna Daniell | Anne Langston | Anthony Bachman | Anthony Palmieri | Anthony R Kurkowski | Barry Deutsch | Ben Hess | Benjamin Mialot | Bill Boehmer | Bill Kong | Blake Petit | Bob Gilson | Bobby Timony | Bradley D. Johnson | Brandon James | Brandon Peterson | Brandon Wagner | Brent Kossina | Brian Freesh | Brian J. Crowley | Brian Kong | Brian Miller | Brian Miller | Brian Tabor | Bruce Macintosh | Caitlin Hier | Cameron Moore | Cameron Scott | Caoimhe Snow | Carl Rigney | Caryn Stardancer | Catie Coleman | Chad Jones | Chantaal Elliot | Charlie Mcelvy | Cheryl Dury | Cheryl Trooskin-Zoller | Chris Greathouse | Chris Ivey | Chris Neseman | Chris Schmitz | Chriscross | Christian Vilaire | Christina Pressner | Christine Ditzel | Christopher C. Cockrell | Christopher Kelly | Chuck Rizor | Chuck Suffel | Cindy Womack | Colin Miskowitz | Conor Kilpatrick | Courtland Funke | Craig Gordon | D.j. Cole | Dabian Witherspoon | Dan Hentschel | Dan Mishkin | Daniel Logan | Daniel M. Clark | Daniel Theodore | Darrell Taylor | Darwin Pierce | David Amore | David Bernstein | David Cederberg | David Golbitz | David Gold | David Malone | David Marquez | David Moore | David Salomon | David Walker | David Wendt | David Weter | Devin Mckenna | Diarra Harris | Don Cromie | Donald Cantwell | Donny Davis | Doug Smidebush | Drew Bittner | Dylan Cassard | Ed Matuskey | Elizabeth Woodard | Emmanuel Pleshe | Eric Newgard | Ericka Culbertson | Erik Scott | Erin Duell | Erin Prather Stafford | Francisco Bonilla | Francisco Rivera | Fred Hicks | Gabriel Cassata | Gaz Gretsky | Gemma Laity | George Tramountanas | Greg Pak | Gregory Morrow | Gretchen Kolderup | Guy Mclimore | Gwendolyn Mary Clay | Hassan Thalji | Heather Donahue | Heidi Foland | Henry Benton | Hilary Goldstein | Holli Mintzer | Ian Levenstein | J.k.woodward | Jack Gulick | Jack Lawrence | Jackson Baumgartner | Jacob Shumaker | Jacob Welch | Jake Wilson | Jameel Alkhafiz | James Allan | James Heffron | James Tichy | Jamie Dallessandro | Janna O'shea | Jared Axelrod | Jason Bergman | Jason Blankenship | Jason Crase | Jason Fliegel | Jason Kruse | Jason L Blair | Jason M Eller | Jason Wood | Jay Faerber | Jay Leisten | Jb Balen | Jd Calderon | Jeff Barbanell | Jeff Petersen | Jeffrey D. Pegues | Jen & Joe Kleinhenz | Jerry Livengood | Jesse Garcia | Jesse Morgan | Jim Burrows | Jim Calafiore | Jim Fenner | Jim Waters | Joe Martino | Joe Regalado | John A. Judd | John Burkhart | John D. Roberts | John Mounter | John Newquist | John Portley | John Williams | John Williams | Jon Plummer | Jonathan Petersen | Jonathan Roscetti | Jonny Rice | Jordan Gibson | Jordan Phegley | Jose Barroso | Jose Maisonet-Torres | Joseph Oakes | Josh Rensch | Joshua Atkins | Judy Abbate | Jules Rivera | Julian Lytle | Julian Orr | Justin Adkins | Justin Bumpus-Barnett | Justin Short | Justin Stewart | Karl Markovich | Kate Kirby | Kate Ledum | Kate Lindsay | Katharine Kan | Katie Hutchins | Keith Chan | Kerry Frey | Kevin D. Hendricks | Kevin Huxford | Kevin Lee | Khalid Birdsong | Kimberly Poole | Kirk Chen | Kong | Kora Bongen | L Jamal Walton | Laura Burns | Laura Miello | Lauren Harris | Leah Webber | Les Rosenthal | Lewis Creech | Linda Lee Butler | Lisa Mccarty | Liz Pilecki | Lorenzo Garcia Jr. | Lori Cole | Luke Foster | Lydia Eickstaedt | Malcolm Kodi Colmer | Mandi Arthur-Struss | Marc Hammond | Marc Marcelo | Margaret Richter | Mark Cooper | Mark Katzoff | Mark Kraus | Mark Kriegsman | Mason Kramer | Matt Kramer | Matt Martinez | Matt Miner | Matt Riggsby | Matthew Wang | Megan Bartelt | Melanie Nazelrod | Meredith Gillies | Michael A. Burstein | Michael Gomez | Michael Gonzalez | Michael Myers | Michael Pfefferkorn | Michael Schwartz | Michele Jeleniewski | Mike Edmundson | Mike Negin | Mike Ortiz | Mike Wickliff | Miriam And Emma Peterson | Molly Jones | Myron Rumsey | Nate Lovett | Nathan Bone | Neil Errar | Nestor D. Rodriguez | Nick Allen | Nick Newman | Nick Nunes | Nick Wesselmann | Octavio Arango | Pamela Milwid | Patrick A. Reed | Patrick Graney | Patrick Rennie | Patrick Williams | Paul Allor | Paul Benjamin | Paul Deatherage | Paul Milligan | Paul Zenisek | Pete Woods | Peter Glanville | Phillip Suttkus | Quentin Rowe | Rachael Rossman | Radley Masinelli | Randall Wright | Randy Golden | Randy Lander | Ray Long | Rebecca Hall | Renee Carignan | Richard Brassell | Richard Bruning | Richard Gilmore | Richard Vu | Rick Wood | Rikki White | Rob Anderson | Rob Tevis | Robbie Holmes | Robert Greenberger | Robert Guadagno | Robert Huss | Robert Picard | Ryan Fedon | Ryan Schrodt | Ryan Thurlow | Samuel Crider | Sara Giometti | Sarah Schanze | Savanna Arevalo | Scott Bradley | Scott Havens | Scott Martin | Scott Milstein | Scott Santos | Scott Slemmons | Scott Stenlake | Scott Weinstein | Sean Frost | Sean Hopkins | Sean Mcardle | Sean Williams | Shag Matthews | Shane K. Mulholland | Shane Sarte | Shannon Reynolds | Shaun Manning | Shawn Kittelsen | Shawn Mckinney | Shawn Mcloughlin | Shawn Pryor | Shoshana Bailar | Sienna Chin Gerding | Simon Fraser | Stephen Brown | Steve Conley | Steve Ekstrom | Steve Ellis | Steve Flack | Steve Garfield | Steve Sullivan | Steve Sunu | Steven E Gordon | Steven Henderson | Suzanne Andora Barron | T.c. Ford | Tamara Brooks | Tamara Hodge | Ted Brown | Tim Kiser | Tom Stillwell | Tommy Bort | Tommy Lewis | Tracy Smith | Travis Moore | Valerie Gillis | Vanity Espinosa | Victoria Donnelly | Vinnie Bartilucci | Vito Delsante | Wendi Freeman | William Beisswanger | William English | William Pardlow | William Rosado | Zachary A. Davino | Ben Hess | Silvia Salinas | Cameron Hatheway | James Turnbull | Jennifer Primosch | Justin Gray | Marie Steel | Mark Mckenna | Paul Jenkins | Peter Bonavita | Raz Solo | Shauna Field | Steve Mannion | Tami Martin | Vincent Povirk | Allen Wright | Janine Frederick | Wilmar Luna, Iii | Justin Korthof | Achmad Sirman | Alan Wilkinson | Amy Goodwin | Andreas Beck | Andria White | Anne-Marie Carslaw | Anthony Hazell | Anthony Madden | Audie Norman | Barbara Kesel | Beth Scorzato | Bill Walko | Brent Schoonover | Brian | Brian Carloni | Brian Letendre | Brian Macdonald | Brooke Schlottke | Bruce Patnaude | Bryan Ash | Carla Mann | Carolyn Atkins | Carolyn Paplham | Charles D Chenet | Charlie Kirchoff | Charlie Twist | Chris Beckett | Chris Buchheit | Chris Engle | Chris Shields | Christian Steinmetz | Christopher Daley | Clarence Riley | Cole Ott | Dan Bodenstein | Dan Spigarolo | David | David Gill | David Medinnus | David Oliva | David Price | David Sylvis | David Weisman | Dean Stahl | Dmajor7th | Drew Close | Drew Mowry | Edward Ainsworth | Edward W Sizemore | Elise Thrasher | Erin M. Hartshorn | Evan D. Jones | Garrick Ellison | Gill Stokes | Helen Mclean | Irrevenant | Ivan Velez | J.c. Hutchins | Jacques Massard | James Babbo | Jari Uimonen | Jayle Enn | Jeff Linder | Jeff Metzner | Jenna Hull | Jenni Simmons | Jenny Jones | Jeremy Spurlock | Jesse Matonak | Jimi Bonogofsky | Jo-Herman Haugholt | Joey Nazzari | John Bedovian | John Nacinovich | John Rogers | Jordan Nicholson | Joseph Lewis | K.c. Solano | Kai Charles | Karl Jahn | Kellen Wolfe | Kenny Keil | Kirt Dankmyer | Korby Marks | Lara Fan | Laura Martin | Laura Morley | Leila Del Duca | Likeabox | Lionel Ruland | Lisa Martincik | Lori Feldman | Lori Lum | Mandi Odo | Martin Rudat | Mathieu Doublet | Matt Board | Matt Goldey | Matthew | Matthew Cranor | Menachem Luchins | Michael Bowman | Michael Sarrao | Mike Zipser | Miriam Saphra | Mitch Gerads | Montserrat | Mordechai Luchins | Morgan Piatt | Nate Cosby | Olivia Von Kohorn | Owen Phelps | Paul Jan | Paul Storrie | Paul Was | Phil Lamarr | R David Murray | Rachelle Stein | Rafael De Cerqueira Sanches Saraiva | Rebecca Hb. | Ricardo Amaral Filho | Rich Hardy | Rob M. Worley | Rob Mcmonigal | Robin Riggs | Rodrigo Dos Reis Cabral | Ronda Grizzle | Ryan Closs | Ryan Dunlavey | Ryan Nardiello | Ryan Nellis | Samax Randolph | Sandy Antunes | Sarah Singer | Scott Christian Sava | Scott Saternye | Scott Suehle | Shawn Deloache | Stephen Loiaconi | Steve Lieber | Steven Goldman | Suzanne Diazmoran | Tad Kelson | Thane Benson | Thomas Bourke | Tim Talbert | Tony Nelson | Travis Thomas | Tyler Leto | Valerie Juarez | Vivian Tynes | Walt Grogan | Wayne Cordova | William Hodge | William Wested | Yenny Coll | Zach Cole | Zachary Dorman | Lance Roger Axt | Aaron Kashtan | Aaron Lopez | Anna Mcallister | Antonio Rocha | Carlos Carmona | Chad Cole | Chris Guillebeau | Dominique Agri | Eric Grau | Gil Colon | James Mcnichols | Jarreau Wimberly | Jay Scott | Jim Ryan | Josie Campbell | K. Ann Sulaiman | Kwanza Johnson | Kyle Horner | Lauren Miller | Lizard-Socks | Matt Ranard | Molly Craycroft | Poet Mase | Rich Douek | Sara Denunzio | Sean Von Gorman | Travers Cleeman | Zen | **THANK YOU!**

MOLLY DANGER
Book One

First Edition, 2013

JAMAL IGLE writer & penciller
JUAN CASTRO inker
ROMULO FAJARDO Jr. colorist
FRANK CVETKOVIC letterer
JAMAL IGLE cover
ADAM P. KNAVE editor
KARINE IGLE graphic design
CATHERINE IGLE inspiration & distraction

Printed on 128 Gsm Gold East Matte Art Paper
Berthold Akzidenz Grotesk font

Published by **Action Lab Entertainment, inc.**
Canonsburg, PA
www.actionlabcomics.com

Printed in China by **Global PSD**
980 Lincoln Ave Suite 200 B San Rafael, CA 94901

ISBN: 978-1-939352-40-8